Philosophical
Resources
for Christian
Thought

Philosophical Resources for Christian Thought

Edited and with an Introductory Essay by Perry LeFevre

ABINGDON PRESS Nashville—New York

Contents

Contents

1 | Perry LeFevre | Theology and Philosophy in the Recent Past — an Introductory Essay

Many have observed that we have come to the end of an era in theology. The giants are departing the scene. The impact of their theological work is certainly not exhausted, but new voices are being heard, and they appear to be singing new songs. No one is sure what direction the contemporary mood in theology may take, but one may guess that the relationship between Christian thought and philosophy will be approached in fresh ways. It may well be that, on the American scene at least, Christian thinkers will find a greater resource in philosophy than the dominant theological climate of the recent past has seemed to allow. It was with something of this kind of conviction that the Chicago Theological Seminary planned this 1966 series of Alden-Tuthill Lectures and invited Charles Hartshorne, Quentin Lauer, S.J., Frederick Ferré, and John Macquarrie to address themselves to the theme "Philosophical Resources for Christian Thought." The Seminary singled out process philosophy, phenomenology, linguistic analysis, and existentialism as those types of philosophical thought most likely to play a part in Christian thinking in the days ahead.

7

"Christian thought" is a broader term than "Christian theology"; but even as we consider the possible contribution of philosophy to Christian thought in the broader sense, it may not be amiss to take a backward look, to give a summary analysis of the way in which the relationship between theology and philosophy was conceived by the dominant theological writers of the closing era. Indeed, the relationship between theology in the narrower sense and philosophy is likely to control judgments as to the possible contribution of philosophy, or even perhaps of all secular wisdom, to the whole spectrum of Christian thought.

The general impression shared by many is that the ascendant theology of the past four decades has been unequivocally hostile to philosophy. Is this true? And have the major theologians of this period of our history spoken with a single voice on the relationship between theology and philosophy? A review of these issues may help give perspective to the shifting winds of theological interpretation. It is with this hope that we examine the views of four of the major theologians of our time: Karl Barth, Emil Brunner, Rudolf Bultmann, and Paul Tillich.

KARL BARTH

No single theologian has done more to shape the prevailing theological climate of the last four decades

than Karl Barth. From the second edition of his com-
mentary on *The Epistle to the Romans* (1921) which
"fell like a bomb on the playground of the theologians" [1]
Barth moved steadily toward the development of a
theology of the Word based exclusively on the biblical
witness. His work in this first decade did not clearly
disclose what was to be his mature judgment about the
relationship of theology to philosophy. His writings show
the influence of his study of Plato, Kant, and
Kierkegaard. His first effort in dogmatics, which
he called *Christian Dogmatics,* seemed to him to
need radical reworking almost by the time it was in
print, in order to cut off any dependency of theology
upon philosophy or upon a general anthropological
approach. By 1932, when he explained in the Foreword
to his new *Church Dogmatics* one of the significant
differences between this work and the earlier one, he
wrote: "To the best of my ability I have cut out in this
second issue of the book everything that in the first
issue might give the slightest appearance of giving to
theology a basis, support, or even a mere justification
in the way of existential philosophy." [2] To move in the
earlier direction he now felt would mean the readoption
of the line of nineteenth-century theology, and he de-

[1] Karl Adam cited by J. McConnachie, *The Significance of Karl
Barth* (London: Hodder & Stoughton, 1931), p. 42.
[2] *Church Dogmatics* (Edinburgh: T. & T. Clark, 1936), I/1, ix.

9

clared, "In any thinkable continuation of this line I can only see the plain destruction of Protestant theology and the Protestant Church." [3] Furthermore he repudiated the Roman Catholic approach to a natural knowledge of God based on the analogy of being, stating: "I regard the *analogia entis* as the invention of Antichrist." [4]

It would be a mistake, however, to take such statements as a simple repudiation of philosophy. In an essay published in 1929, "Schicksal und Idee in der Theologie" ("Destiny and Idea in Theology") there is perhaps an important clue to the direction his thought was taking as to the proper relation between theology and philosophy. Here Barth points out that theology and philosophy operate in a common area of concern. The problems posed by the conflict between philosophical realism and philosophical idealism, the one with its emphasis on objective reality and givenness, the other with its emphasis on truth or, to put it another way, the relation of the nongiven (spirit or thought) to the given, are shared by theology. Theology has to deal with the same issues, but theology must do so theologically, not philosophically. The presumption of philosophy that it can reach the ultimate by starting either from given objective reality or from thought must be rejected by theology. Neither path is possible, for man is a sinner.

[3] *Ibid.*, x.
[4] *Ibid.*

10

He can only acknowledge God when God addresses him. Therefore, there must be a strict boundary between what the theologian must assume and what the philosopher assumes. The philosopher is not to give up "doing philosophy"; but the theologian must deny the possibility of "doing theology" as a philosopher.

In the course of his massive *Church Dogmatics* Barth continues to clarify and to elaborate his view of the relations between theology and philosophy. The emphasis on the basic autonomy of theology is extended, but there is an acknowledgment of the part philosophical thinking plays in the theologian's task of understanding the Scripture. Barth states clearly that an objective understanding of the text cannot come apart from a subjective realizing of it in our own thinking. We cannot "free ourselves of our own shadow." [5] Each of us will approach "the text from the standpoint of a particular epistemology, logic or ethics, of definite ideas and ideals concerning the relations of God, the world and man, and . . . in reading and expounding the text he cannot simply deny these." [6] Barth goes on to say: "Everyone has some sort of philosophy, i.e., a personal view of the fundamental nature and relationship of things—however popular, aphoristic, irregular and eclectically vacillating." [7] In-

[5] *Ibid.*, I/2, 727.
[6] *Ibid.*, 728.
[7] *Ibid.*

11

deed, even the most sophisticated theories of biblical ex-
position have philosophical antecedents. The Bible is
never allowed to speak solely for itself. It is always read
through the spectacles of a world view:

If we hold up hands of horror at the very idea, we must
not forget that without such systems of explanation, without
such spectacles, we cannot read the Bible at all. It is, therefore, a grotesque comedy, in which it is better not to take
part, that again and again there are those who think that
they can point with outstretched finger to all others past
and present, accusing them of falling victim to this or that
philosophy, while they themselves abide wholly by the
facts, relying on their two sound eyes. No one does that,
for no one can. It is no more true of anyone that he does
not mingle the Gospel with some philosophy, than that here
and now he is free from all sin except through faith.[8]

The use of philosophy is not only legitimate but also
unavoidable. The question however is how philosophy
is used. One who uses philosophy must in the first
place be fully aware of what he is doing. Secondly, he
must use the philosophy as a kind of hypothesis, in an
exploratory, experimental, and provisional manner. To
do this, one must bear in mind that there is a real
difference between Scripture's mode of thought and

[8] *Ibid.*, 728-29.

one's own. One's own categories, so to say, are unfit, and moreover different categories may be used by others. Furthermore, one must realize that the system of thought we bring to exegesis can claim no independent interest. The danger is that we shall put our scheme of thought on the same level as Scripture. No philosophy should become an absolute, a norm alongside Scripture. In the fourth place, says Barth, there is no essential reason for giving preference to one philosophical perspective over all others. In the history of interpretation various approaches have been fruitful through the grace of the Word. Finally, the use of philosophy must be a critical use, that is, the text and what the text mirrors must be in control, and the scheme of thought contribute to reflection. In words which he later echoes in *Credo,* Scripture must not become a captive to any human scheme of thought.[9]

Another point at which Barth's attitude toward philosophy and the relation between theology and philosophy receives further elaboration is in his treatment of anthropology. Barth's earlier discussion and his abandonment of the *Christian Dogmatics* made clear his view that theology could not be grounded in anthropology, and his statement of his own starting point in the Word of God in the first volume of *Church Dog-*

[9] Cf. *Credo* (New York: Scribner's, 1962), pp. 183 ff.

13

matics further confirmed his views as to the fundamental autonomy of theology. One might think, however, that, though theology must both begin and return to the Word of God, the understanding of man's own nature might draw upon philosophical resources, indeed upon resources from the sciences of man as well. When one turns to Barth's treatment of man in volume III of the *Dogmatics,* he finds that Barth repudiates such a possibility. At the heart of Barth's judgment stands the presupposition that no real understanding of man as man, or no understanding of the real man, can be gained unless man is understood in relation to God, and God's relation to man cannot be understood from man's side, from studying the phenomena of the human. The man who wishes to see himself "otherwise than from God" is not the real man, for it is man's relationship to God which makes him man.[10] Though the study of the phenomena of the human, of man as he appears apart from God, as science, ethics, or even existential philosophy may attempt it, may be "relevant, interesting, important and legitimate"—we cannot expect to get in these ways to "the real definition of man." [11] Barth spends some pages trying to establish his case; in the light of our concern with the relation between theology and philosophy, his judgment about Karl Jaspers as a

[10] *Church Dogmatics,* III/2, 75.
[11] *Ibid.,* 79.

14

representative of existential philosophy is most instructive.

To ask about the existence of man appears to get us
deeper into the problem of man, for it is to ask about the
problem of the subject. It is to go further than science or
ethics. "If we ask concerning existence and therefore
about man as subject, we ask concerning something
which lies essentially outside any theory of man and
therefore outside all possibilities of understanding and
controlling man." [12] To go beyond the objectified self, to
the self itself in its very act of self transcendence, appears
to be getting closer to the real man. Jaspers' theory is that
in the frontier situations (i.e., suffering, death, conflict,
guilt) existence is transformed from a possibility into
actuality and man is met by a transcendence which,
though it will disappear again, nevertheless "will not
fail to greet man, to set its mark upon him, to make his
self-consciousness, which in itself can only be his self-
questing, a cypher or symbol of itself, and therefore of the
man he seeks." [13] Is not this experience of openness, and
of actual relatedness to this transcendent other, the experience of man's real existence?

Barth is willing to grant that a new dimension of
man's life is disclosed by what Jaspers points to—the his-
toricity of man and his relatedness to another, but he will

[12] *Ibid.*, 110.
[13] *Ibid.*, 112.

not grant that Jaspers has shown us the real man. His reason is that there is no real assurance that transcendence meets us in such situations. Specific and particularly negative situations are not intrinsically bearers of the mystery of transcendence and therefore of human life. Moreover, even when man seems to have the experience of transcendence in such situations, there is no guarantee that it is genuine transcendence which meets us. Might it not be a demon? Barth asks. Furthermore, the view that when a man meets the other in such moments with unconditional trust, he will be freed from anguish and find that perfect peace does not exhaust the alternatives. Man may very well meet the other with "a conditional surrender limited by our own defiance." [14] If it were genuine transcendence that meets us one would think man could not choose this second alternative. But there is still another alternative. The assertion that human life is related to transcendence, Barth says, presupposes that man is interested in himself—that he is seeking his true self. But is resignation not another possibility? Are there not weary and indifferent men?

But Barth does not halt his critique at this point. The underlying assumption in these existentialist views is that man can decide to turn in unconditional faith and absolute trust to the other. They assume that man has the capacity to trust unconditionally, that it is already

[14] *Ibid.*, 116.

16

within him. To assume so is to assume that he has transcendence within, and that transcendence and existence are one and the same. Barth concludes:

Unmistakably, even though against the intention and the purpose of this anthropology, we are again confronted by the picture of a self-enclosed human reality beyond which there is nothing to confront it, and which, because it is itself the one and all, cannot be confronted by anything that might be identified with the God who is distinct from man and the world, and superior to both.[15]

From the side of philosophy, then, even in what might be thought to be its most promising form so far as theology is concerned, there can come no contribution to a genuine understanding of the real man, if the real man is man in relation to genuine transcendence.

It is interesting that Barth's brother Heinrich is a distinguished existentialist philosopher. The philosopher Barth saw in the philosophical concept of existence not the possibility of the knowledge of God but merely an analogy to the knowledge of God. The theologian Barth declares that the responsibility for the assertion that in the transcending knowledge of man's existence we have an analogy to knowledge of God, can only be left to the philosopher. Such an assertion cannot be a theological

[15] *Ibid.*, 119.

proposition. In any case, such an analogy cannot be an anticipatory one but must be a recapitulatory one, seen from the perspective of already revealed truth.[16]

Perhaps Karl Barth's most generous discussion of the broad question of the relationship of theology and philosophy is his recent contribution to the *Festschrift* for his brother, entitled *Philosophie und christliche Existenz*. Barth's own essay is called simply "Philosophy and Theology." [17]

In this essay Barth says that somewhere and somehow the philosopher and the theologian, each in his own work, will have to deal with the problems of the other. What distinguishes the one from the other is the difference as to which problem is primary. In their relationship they should both think of themselves as standing before the whole truth, as being fellowmen to each other, sharing the responsibility of this confrontation. Each must be concerned about the whole truth, but each in his own way.

Both theology and philosophy are human enterprises. Neither can possess the whole truth. Both can only attempt to serve it, to place themselves at its disposal. The philosopher and the theologian will follow different ways; they will engage in controversy, but

[16] *Ibid.,* I/1, 42-43.

[17] *Philosophie und christliche Existenz, Festschrift für Heinrich Barth.* Herausgegeben von Gerhard Huber (Basel und Stuttgart: Verlag Helbing & Lichtenhahn, 1960).

neither can claim superiority over the other in any final sense. There are two problems which are central in each discipline, two "moments" of the one entire truth. The philosopher will give primacy to one, the theologian to the other. For the theologian the two moments might be called: Creator and creature, God's freedom for man and man's freedom given by God. For theology, primacy lies in God the Creator. Theological work must always begin from God's side. For the philosopher the moments seem to be analogous, but the primacy is different. Whether the philosopher uses terms like idea and phenomenon, logos and reason, transcendence and existence, Sein and Dasein, he gives primacy to the human dimension. He starts with man and his life and experience.

Barth raises a question about the apparent parallelism between the terms on the theological side and the philosophical side. Is there a real analogy? Are the theologian and the philosopher speaking about the same realities but simply using different vocabularies? Perhaps an honest probing of the issue would disclose that an integration of the vocabularies is impossible or perhaps it might be otherwise. But the real issue is not the conflict over words. It is rather the difference in starting point. The question is one of primacy and sequence. What defines theology over against philosophy is that for the theologian the movement must be from God to man, and only then from man to God.

Barth raises the question as to whether a Christian philosophy might be possible. In a weak sense of the term he admits that such an enterprise might be possible. That is, the philosopher might be at least alarmed or worried about the direction of theological thinking. But if a philosopher really took seriously the sequence of thought pursued by the theologian, no matter what vocabulary he used, it would be more accurate to call him a crypto-theologian than a Christian philosopher.

From the theologian's perspective there can be no other primacy or sequence. He can only be surprised that the philosopher approaches matters differently. For the theologian, Jesus Christ is the one entire truth, and therefore there is no other path for theology. He will be surprised that, now that all other ways are obsolete, anyone would want to go from man to God, for God himself has come to man. Nevertheless, even in their opposition, nothing can change the fact that the philosopher and the theologian are together as human beings. How should their necessary coexistence be maintained in human dignity? Barth's answer is: they should remain within hearing of each other. They should pay serious attention to each other, even if only to see what is ordered and what is forbidden from each side. It could even happen, he says, that each might learn from the other, even though this can never mean that the one follows the other's way.

The philosopher may learn, for example, something

of the phenomenon of "religion" and of the need to give a proper place to what is meant by faith and revelation. But the theologian will understand these things from his own perspective and the philosopher from his own. And the theologian, while not leaving his own starting point, may still come to admire the philosopher as a careful interpreter of man's self-understanding, to admire him as a worldly wise man, in the best sense of that term. God acted through Christ *for the world.* The theologian should remember this, and perhaps the philosopher may help him to remember it, especially if he should be treating the second "moment" or problem too casually. The philosopher may help him to take nature, culture, and humanity more seriously. And yet the theologian must be careful lest he let philosophy be the devil's advocate and lure him from his primary task. Yet again, it may be Jesus Christ, the Light, Lord, and Savior of the world, who through the worldly wise philosopher calls him to pay attention to the world in a theological way. Theologians and philosophers may therefore coexist, and, though they understand each other each one from his own perspective and so in a sense misunderstand each other, they may coexist in hope. And if, in addition, they also want to be Christians, perhaps, says Barth, they will succeed in the sense of Psalm 133 which his own father used to quote: "Behold, how good and pleasant it is when brothers dwell in unity!"

21

EMIL BRUNNER

In the first decade of the revolt against liberal theology the names of Barth and Brunner were often joined together. For Americans Brunner, because of personal visits to America and English translations of his works, was the chief mediator of the new evangelical theology. Yet as Barth broke ever more clearly any ties to philosophy, the distinctiveness of the two men's positions became apparent. The sharp debate over natural theology and the possibility of a point of contact in man for the reception of revelation only brought this separation to the attention of a wider public.[18] Both the similarities and the differences regarding the relation of theology to philosophy will become clear as we examine Brunner's position.

At the heart of Brunner's view is his understanding of the difference between the truth which lies at the basis of theology and the truth which philosophy seeks and finds. Scientific and philosophical knowledge are grounded in the subject-object dichotomy. The truth from which theology starts transcends the subject-object distinction; it is truth as encounter. Truth as encounter is personal, not impersonal; it is disclosed by being given, not by being sought. It is a happening, not

[18] *Natural Theology. Comprising "Nature and Grace" by Professor Dr. Emil Brunner and the Reply "No!" by Dr. Karl Barth* (London: Geoffrey Bles, 1946).

a deduction or an inference. It comes to man as a being known, not as a knowing initiated by man. It is a being grasped in faith, not a deliberation of reason. Philosophy, even the existentialist philosophy which attempts to overcome the subject-object dichotomy by beginning with existence, cannot reach such truth, for it starts with man alone. In this general viewpoint Brunner appears to be at one with Barth; but when Brunner examines the actual functions of philosophical reason, taken either by itself or under the control of Christian revelation, important differences appear. Brunner wishes to acknowledge a more positive role for reason taken alone and to make a specific place for what he calls Christian philosophy within the framework of theology.

One might sum up Brunner's estimate of the possible role of philosophical reason untouched by the revelation of Jesus Christ by saying that at the most it may bear the relation of law to gospel. For example, he grants that knowledge of the moral law is possible for human reason as such, but the moral reason is limited: "in the incapacity to determine whence this law comes, in the incapacity to know evil in its depths, in the abstract nature of the demand, and in its impotence to overcome resistance." [19] All these incapacities are overcome in the encounter with Christ. So, too, rational theology, whether in its proofs for the existence of God

[19] Emil Brunner, *Revelation and Reason* (Philadelphia: The Westminster Press, 1946), p. 326.

23

or in its speculative metaphysical systems, *may* at best disclose "something of the original revelation of God in the human mind." They show that in "the human mind itself there is something transcendent, an immanent transcendence, which constrains man, when he reflects upon himself, to go beyond himself." [20] But such immanent facts—the ideas of the good, the true, and the perfect—"are not sufficient to teach man to know *God*." [21] And within a culture permeated by Christian notions they may get their power only from their connection with their Christian roots. Of course, rational speculation may not lead even to this qualified positive result. It can lead farther and farther away toward agnosticism or positivism. And in no case can such approaches be a substitute for faith. They do not lead to truth as encounter which is saving knowledge. Yet there is one form of rational philosophical thought about God which Brunner comes closer to approving than any other. This he calls philosophical theism. Historically speaking, theistic philosophy, Brunner says, exists only within the Christian sphere: "it is the philosophical doctrine of God, which develops in agreement with the Christian faith, but—either in intention or actually—from rational motives." "With a slight exaggeration," he says, "we may say that philosophical Theism is identi-

[20] *Ibid.*, p. 344.
[21] *Ibid.*, p. 345.

cal with Christian philosophy." [22] Though the human mind may find elevation in such rational theology, "it will not find in it the 'truth which makes us free,' it will not be able to recognize the God who wills to realize His Kingdom." [23] Such thinking may in fact be dangerous—one may lose both, the rational basis of argument and the truth of revelation.

Nevertheless, Brunner believes such thinking has a place. Characterizing A. E. Taylor's Gifford Lectures as a "blending of rational theistic philosophy, natural theology, Christian philosophy, and Christian theological apologetics," he comments:

It is in the nature of the case that Christian philosophy, when it deals with the problems of religion, offers this aspect. It is wholly injurious, and not in any way fortunate for German Protestantism, that it has practically lost this, for it, important link between philosophy and theology, between the message of the Church and secular knowledge.[24]

What then is Christian philosophy for Brunner? One way of giving Brunner's answer is to say that Christian philosophy is what believing Christians produce when they think philosophically. There can be Christian philosophers just as there can be Christian artists, and any man's work will reflect his Christian

[22] *Ibid.*, p. 358.
[23] *Ibid.*, p. 362.
[24] *Ibid.*, p. 360.

faith. Another way to put it is to say with Brunner that in the area of the knowledge of the created world many problems are specialist problems which are to be dealt with by reason alone. Other problems, and they arise the closer they come to "that center of existence where we are concerned with the whole, that is, with man's relation to God and the being of the person," [25] demand a correction of purely rational knowledge by the knowledge of faith. It is to this area that Christian philosophy belongs. Faith is not reason, and faith is not Christian philosophy. But neither is theology faith. Theology is thought about the content of divine revelation as such. It is the explication of the great themes of the Bible and above all about "that which has been revealed to us through and about Jesus Christ." [26] Christian philosophy deals with those important border problems where autonomous reason is not fully competent and where what is known through faith makes a difference in the interpretation of the created order. Thus says Brunner:

The difference between the Christian theologian and the Christian who, without forgetting his faith, reflects upon the problems of time and eternity, necessity and freedom, the individual and the community, is merely a difference of subject, not of method. The difference between Christian

[25] *Ibid.*, p. 383.
[26] *Ibid.*, p. 385.

philosophy and Christian theology is therefore not one of principle, but it is a fluid transition.[27]

In this sense, "every 'systematic theologian' . . . is philosopher and theologian in the one person." [28]

A critical question of course arises in relation to thought about God. Is thought about God necessarily theological from a Christian point of view, or can a Christian philosopher reflect on the problem of God? Brunner's answer is not utterly clear. In one of his most recent works Brunner says, "Christian philosophy is the reflection of a believing Christian about being and about existing realities as these are disclosed in experience of the world. It is reflection concerning the principles of being and of thought about being. But it is a thinking that is freed from the illusory prejudice of autonomy." [29] And since Brunner affirms the analogy of being, this might well lead one to conclude that philosophical thought about God is acceptable. Yet he goes on to say that "the God of the Biblical revelation is neither that which is thought, the absolute object, nor the act of thinking, the thinking subject, but the self-revealing and self-communicating Lord of being." [30] This is the living God who is not at the disposal of human thought.

[27] *Ibid.*, p. 390.
[28] *Ibid.*
[29] Emil Brunner, *Truth as Encounter* (Philadelphia: The Westminster Press, 1964), p. 51.
[30] *Ibid.*, p. 52.

This same problem is reflected in the interchange between Brunner and Tillich in the volume on Brunner in the *Library of Living Theology*. Tillich points to the symbolic character of Brunner's personalistic categories for speaking of God and suggests that he could develop a more adequate view if he recognized their symbolic character and developed transpersonal categories. Brunner's response was mixed: "The Systematic Theology of Tillich has to this day not succeeded in convincing me that combining faith in God with philosophical ontology gives an advantage to the former." And yet, "The transformation of Christian faith arising from the introduction of ontological concepts surely has its positive side, for Tillich has thereby caught the ear of the many who reject faith precisely because they regard its personalism as anthropomorphism. . . . It creates, so to speak, an emergency bridge from faith to impersonal rational knowledge or philosophy." [31]

If we return for clarification to Brunner's *Truth as Encounter*, we see that it is perhaps not ontology that Brunner opposes but particular kinds of ontology. He points out that philosophers have often identified the revealed God with Absolute Being, and he writes: "The neutral impersonal or transcendent existent which is the highest, most abstract thought of philosophical

[31] *The Theology of Emil Brunner*, ed. by Charles W. Kegley ("The Library of Living Theology," Vol. III [New York: The Macmillan Company, 1962]), pp. 334-35.

speculation, has nothing to do with the 'living God' of faith. . . . The first task of Christian philosophy consists in showing that the concept of the divine Being has nothing to do with this ontology of the *summum bonum,* but excludes it in principle. The true ontology is rather that of the absolutely free, self-determining will, which is determined by nothing but its own willing." [32] Some further support for such an interpretation of Brunner's meaning is found in his listing of a large number of those whom he considers to be "real Christian philosophers," such as Augustine, Pascal, Hamann, Kierkegaard, Edwards, Vinet, Secretan, Royce, Guardini, von Hügel, Bevan, *et al.* Certainly many of these men developed philosophical conceptions of God which went beyond biblical categories.

RUDOLF BULTMANN

The name of Rudolf Bultmann, like that of Emil Brunner, was closely associated by many with that of Karl Barth in the first decade of the new theological revolution. The difference between Bultmann and Barth soon became clear and ultimately became so sharp that a recent writer speaks of Barth and Bultmann as representing "the divided mind of modern theology." "What

[32] *Truth as Encounter,* pp. 52-53.

should be two poles of Christian thought has become two irreconcilable theological movements" with Bultmann and his followers in one and Barth and his followers in the other.[33] A most significant part of the difference between the two rests upon their radically different views as to the relation between theology and philosophy.

In an important sense Bultmann stands for a much more positive role for philosophy in its connection with theology than either Barth or Brunner. Unlike Brunner he does not call for a Christian philosophy. Rather he calls for the theologian's positive use of philosophy as an autonomous discipline in relation to his own theological work. At the same time he refuses to collapse theology into philosophy of any kind. Beneath Bultmann's efforts to spell out the relationship of theology and philosophy there lies a fundamental conviction about the very basis of Christian theology. Theology presupposes the exclusive act of God in Christ disclosed only to faith. This act of God gives a direct and personal knowledge of God's relation to the particular man who responds in faith, and it transforms his self-understanding. All knowledge which does not come through faith in response to Jesus Christ is not knowledge of God as God. This means that all objectifying knowledge of God is really not knowledge of God at all, for God can be known only through the

[33] James D. Smart, *The Divided Mind of Modern Theology* (Philadelphia: The Westminster Press, 1967), p. 8.

faith that transforms man's own self-understanding. For Bultmann philosophy cannot reach knowledge of God.

What then is the role of philosophy? Can it be of any help to the theologian? Faith represents a transformed self-understanding. It is a new self-understanding. The task of the theologian is to find a way of conceptualizing this new self-understanding which in the past has been carried by the mythological language of the Bible. The mythological language of the Bible not only stands in the way of adequate communication and conceptualization because modern man does not find it meaningful, but it is a language of objectification. In order to express man's understanding of himself and his world, it objectifies the transcendent reality which faith knows, contradicting the very point which faith itself establishes, i.e., that this transcendent reality cannot be known as an object or spoken about in object language. What appears under the guise of myth as objective talk about God must, since God cannot be conceptualized or turned into an object, be translated into talk about that mode of existence which faith is. Theology thus involves the existential interpretation of myth, or, as Bultmann calls it, demythologization. Theology is the clarification of existence in faith, the true meaning of which was indirectly expressed in biblical myth. The exegete must get behind what is apparently being said to what is really being said concerning man's self-understanding. Bultmann believes that the basis for such existential interpretation is to be found in philosophy. Thus the theologian becomes dependent upon the philosopher's interpretation of existence for what is at the center of his task as theologian.

Though exegesis must become subordinate to the work of the philosopher, this does not mean for Bultmann that either theology or exegesis becomes subordinate to a particular world view. In order to understand this distinction, which has apparently been unclear to some of his critics, one must understand what Bultmann means by philosophy. With respect to what faith discloses, philosophy, as Bultmann understands it, is neutral. Philosophy is concerned with general structures. Both theology and philosophy can deal with man, but philosophy inquires "ontologically into the formal structures of human existence," while theology speaks of "the concrete man insofar as he is faithful (or is unfaithful—which is also something positive and not negative), i.e., insofar as his 'how' is characterized by the fact that he has been or is to be encountered by a specific proclamation." [34] Because philosophy is concerned with these general structures, theology must use its conceptualizations (which deal with the possibilities of human existence) to express the meaning of that particular possibility of human existence which is life in faith. To put it another way, every interpreter of the biblical text is in-

[34] Rudolf Bultmann, *Existence and Faith* (New York: Living Age Books, 1960), p. 94.

escapably dependent on the concepts of some philosophy or other. Critical and reflective consideration will lead the exegete to find the most adequate terminology or conceptuality. The critical exegete will try to find the "right" philosophy. Bultmann believes that existential philosophy, particularly that of Heidegger, is that "right" philosophy. For in *Being and Time*, Heidegger makes the understanding of human existence central. Yet again Bultmann believes that theology does not thereby become identical with philosophy. He writes of Heidegger: "I learned from him not *what* theology has to say, but *how* it has to say it, in order to speak to the thinking man today in a way that he can understand." [35] A theology which does not try to make its understanding of man conceptually explicit by trying to get concepts that express the meaning of the being of man in the most appropriate and neutral way possible and which does not ask philosophy for such a conceptuality is "a mere fake." [36] To fail to do this is to be uncritically dependent on some older philosophical tradition or to become a philosopher oneself in some hidden way.

Philosophy thus provides the general categories or thought forms about existence within which the particular understanding gained in faith can be interpreted by theology. Thus the neutral and general

[35] *The Theology of Rudolf Bultmann*, ed. by Charles W. Kegley (New York: Harper & Row, 1966), p. 276.
[36] *Existence and Faith*, p. 98.

category of man's being toward the future is the philosophical conception within which the particular Christian understanding of existence in terms of eschatology can be placed. The general ontological notion of guilt is the basis for speaking of sin as a Christian category. The understanding of the "care" structure of existence is the basis for interpreting the Christian notion of love. Philosophy provides the indispensable analysis of the general structures of human existence within which and by means of which every specific personal self-understanding would have to be set forth.

Though philosophy as Bultmann understands it is critically important for the task of theology, namely, the clarification of existence in faith, it is just as critically limited in what it can provide. According to Bultmann it can never be a substitute for theology, nor can it contribute the real substance for theological reflection. Philosophy can provide the general structures within which the true meaning of human existence can be expressed, but it can never disclose that true meaning of existence by itself. In Bultmann's judgment there are a number of important reasons for holding that philosophy is limited in this fashion. In the first place, the true meaning of existence comes only through faith, and faith comes through revelation, through direct personal encounter with the kerygmatic Christ. The self-knowledge given involves transformation of the individual's self-understanding, the realization of authentic existence. Bultmann would hold that authentic existence is conceivable apart from Christ, but it is not realizable apart from Christ. Christ gives a new self-understanding —this is the revelatory power of the Christ event. Christ brings authentic existence—this is the grace received in the Christ event. The concrete event of revelation is necessary. But some philosophers who might admit this, would hold that revelation is not limited to the Christ event. It is important to understand that Bultmann's limitation of revelation to the Christ event is to be understood eschatologically, that is, it is not to be understood as a miracle that *once* happened, "but as an eschatological happening, which, beginning with Jesus, is always present in the words of men proclaiming it to be a human experience." [37] Nevertheless Bultmann does wish to assert the absoluteness of the Christian revelation. He declares that "wherever a revealed faith speaks, it asserts, and must assert, the absoluteness of its revelation, because it regards itself as the true fulfillment of the commandment: 'I am the Lord thy God. . . . Thou shalt have no other gods before me.' " [38] One can always regard such a revealed faith as absurd. But, says Bult-

[37] Karl Jaspers and Rudolf Bultmann, *Myth and Christianity* (New York: The Noonday Press, 1958), p. 69.
[38] *Ibid.*, p. 67.

35

mann, "a man who does, should not talk about revelation." [39] Moreover, it does no good to look here or look
there in the history of religion for alternative instances
of revelation. Revelation is not visible to the human
eye in this way. All that one could find would be
various instances of faith in revelation, not revelation
itself. "For the revelation is revelation only *in actu* and
only *pro me;* it is understood and recognized as such
only in personal decision." [40] In a sense, therefore, to
claim revelation as ground for faith is inevitably an
exclusivist claim.

No more, according to Bultmann, can one support
a view that there is a kind of natural revelation which
can give knowledge of God. There is a kind of revelation
in nature and history. God does speak to man apart from
Christ but in such a way that man's self-assurance and
self-glorying are shattered. In a sense it points to the
emptiness which we cannot fill. It therefore points
toward, though it does not give, the revelation of the
forgiving grace of God in Christ.[41] To be sure, men
seek for God, but the God they find apart from Christ
is not God. Christian faith asserts "that *all answers*
apart from the Christian answer are *illusions*." [42] Such
questions continue to be pressed upon Bultmann, from

[39] *Ibid.,* p. 68.
[40] *Ibid.*
[41] Rudolf Bultmann, *Essays Philosophical and Theological* (New
York: The Macmillan Company, 1955). Cf. p. 118.
[42] *Ibid.,* p. 98.

36

one side or another. The American theologian Schubert Ogden, a major interpreter of Bultmann's thought, has raised the question of the possibility of a truly philosophical theology. He criticizes Bultmann for restricting himself to the categories of Heidegger's philosophy of existence, pointing out that such restriction limits Bultmann to analogy in talking about God, whereas otherwise he might be able to speak directly of God. Ogden thinks that it is possible to speak directly about God without falsely objectifying him.[43] Bultmann responded to this criticism in 1962 with at least a hint of openness toward such a possibility. Perhaps, even by saying that one cannot speak about God as he is in himself, one is implying a certain objective conceptual thinking about God, for in order to say this, there has to be some idea of what God is, e.g., transcendence. Yet Bultmann raises counter questions. He reaches no conclusion, and finally he wonders if perhaps it might be possible to reach a formal definition of God by using the thought of the later Heidegger. He cites Heidegger's judgment that the godless thinking which has given up the traditional metaphysical notion of God as *causa sui* may actually come closer to the divine God. But Bultmann ends in a questioning mood as to whether or how far it is possible

[43] Schubert Ogden, *Christ Without Myth* (New York: Harper & Row, 1961) and "Bultmann's Demythologizing and Hartshorne's Dipolar Theism" in W. L. Reese and E. Freeman, eds., *Process and Divinity* (LaSalle, Ill.: Open Court, 1964), pp. 493 ff.

to develop a notion of God from Heidegger's view of being.[44]

Several years later Ogden again raised his question in discussing "The Significance of Bultmann for Contemporary Theology." This time Bultmann replied with a more definitive statement, which seems to sum up very well his view of the limitations of philosophy:

I do not consider such a philosophical theology possible. It is only possible to make God the object of conceptual thought in so far as the concept "God" can be objectively explicated. Indeed, that must be the case since theology must be able to say what it means when it speaks of God. Theology must therefore clarify in a conceptual way—for example, the concepts of transcendence, of omnipotence, of the presentness of God, the concepts of grace and forgiveness. This cannot mean, however, that theology speaks directly of God and of his activity. It cannot speak of God as he is in himself, but only of what he does for us.[45]

PAUL TILLICH

Of the four giants of the recent theological past, Paul Tillich looked most affirmatively on the reciprocal

[44] Rudolf Bultmann, "Zur Frage einer philosophischen Theologie" in *Einsichten, Festschrift für Gerhard Krüger* (Frankfurt: Klostermann, 1962), pp. 36-39.

[45] *The Theology of Rudolf Bultmann*, ed. by Charles W. Kegley, p. 273.

relationship of philosophy and theology. He saw his own career as lived on the boundary between theology and philosophy: "As a theologian I have tried to remain a philosopher, and vice versa. It would have been easier to abandon the boundary and to choose one or the other. Inwardly this course was impossible for me." [46] Tillich's work before he came to the United States was particularly addressed to the development of a philosophy of culture, science, and religion. Philosophy was understood as a "theory of the principles of meaning," and philosophy of religion relates these principles of meaning "to a theory of the essence of religion." [47] Theology was seen as providing a normative view of religion based on the experience and interpretation of a particular confessional community. After his coming to the United States Tillich devoted himself more fully to explicitly theological work, and as he produced his own systematic theology he came to define carefully the relationship between theology and philosophy.

Like the kerygmatic theologians Barth, Brunner, and Bultmann, Tillich believed that philosophy had a place in understanding the Bible. Philosophy did not, however, in his view, simply provide an unavoidable

[46] Paul Tillich, *On the Boundary* (New York: Scribner's, 1966), p. 58.
[47] Cf. James Luther Adams, *Paul Tillich's Philosophy of Culture, Science, and Religion* (New York: Harper & Row, 1965), chaps. V and VI; esp. p. 259.

linguistic or conceptual background for interpretation, or even a neutral conceptuality for the contemporary interpretation of existence in faith. Philosophy needs to be taken even more seriously by the biblical theologian. In his small book *Biblical Religion and the Search for Ultimate Reality,* Tillich wrote in strong language:

It is infuriating to see how biblical theologians, when explaining the concepts of the Old or New Testament writers, use most of the terms created by the toil of philosophers and the ingenuity of the speculative mind and then dismiss, with cheap denunciations, the work from which their language has been immensely enriched. No theologian should be taken seriously as a theologian, even if he is a great Christian and a great scholar, if his work shows that he does not take philosophy seriously.[48]

In the same book Tillich writes at length of the apparent incongruity between the notions of biblical personalism and the seemingly objective impersonal categories of ontological thinking, and then he demonstrates that, even in the face of a continuing tension between the dramatic and personal symbols of biblical religion and ontological thinking, "each of the biblical symbols drives inescapably to an ontological question and that the

[48] Paul Tillich, *Biblical Religion and the Search for Ultimate Reality* (Chicago: University of Chicago Press, 1955), pp. 7-8.

answers given by theology necessarily contain ontological elements." [49]

The most explicit analysis of the relationship between systematic theology and philosophy given by Tillich is to be found in the first volume of his *Systematic Theology* and in his inaugural lecture at Union Theological Seminary, entitled "Philosophy and Theology." [50] Tillich's understanding of the relationship between philosophy and theology is based on his view of the nature of each discipline. Philosophy is essentially ontology; it asks the question of the structure of being. Even those philosophers who appear to try to avoid the ontological question inevitably presuppose it and assume some particular type of ontology in doing their work. The object of theology, on the other hand, is what concerns us ultimately. What concerns us ultimately must be real; it must be related to being. For Tillich, it cannot be one being among others. "It must be the ground of our being, that which determines our being or not-being, the ultimate and unconditional power of being." [51] And yet such power of being must express itself through

[49] *Ibid.*, p. vii.

[50] Paul Tillich, *Systematic Theology*, I (Chicago: University of Chicago Press, 1951), and Paul Tillich, *The Protestant Era* (Chicago: University of Chicago Press, 1948), chap. VI. Tillich also deals with this subject in his essay "Metaphysics and Theology," *Review of Metaphysics*, X, 1 (September 1956), pp. 57-63.

[51] *Systematic Theology*, I, 21.

the structures of being. Therefore theology and philosophy both are related to the question of being.

Both disciplines are related to the question of being but from different perspectives. Philosophy is interested in the structure of being in itself. Theology is interested in the meaning of being for us. The attitude of the philosopher is more detached and objective, that of the theologian is more existential and involved. Yet even so, all philosophy begins in wonder and is driven by a kind of passion, and the theologian cannot escape the objective problem of the structure of being. Moreover, though the philosopher and the theologian turn to different sources, the one reality as a whole and the structures that appear in it, the other the manifestation of that which concerns him ultimately in the concrete event, and though the content tends to be cosmological on the one hand and soteriological on the other, there is in every philosopher a hidden theologian, and in every theologian a hidden philosopher. Nevertheless, there is no synthesis possible between them, just as there is no conflict, for they lack a common basis, even though there are elements of convergent interest.

Another way to point to the intimate relationship of philosophy and theology in Tillich's view is to speak of his theological method, of what he terms the method of correlation. Theology is the explanation of the Christian faith in a methodical way. It explains the contents of the Christian faith by bringing together man's existential questions and the theological answers. In order to explain the Christian faith, the theologian must therefore formulate the questions which are implied in human existence. This task is a philosophical one, even when it is performed by the theologian. The materials used for formulating the questions are derived from all the realms of culture, including philosophy, but the analysis of existence and of the questions implicit in existence is a philosophical task. In this philosophical analysis of existence theology does not dictate what is to be found. The philosopher, or the theologian as philosopher, proceeds autonomously. He is determined only by what his object is. On the other hand, Tillich asserts that, when the theologian develops the answers to the existential questions, he does not find them in human existence, he finds them given in the symbols of the Christian faith. For Tillich, neither philosopher nor theologian can find "answers" through an analysis of human existence. The answers "are 'spoken' to human existence from beyond it." [52]

---

[52] *Ibid.*, pp. 60 ff.; esp. p. 64.

2 | Charles Hartshorne | Process Philosophy as a Resource for Christian Thought

What shall we mean by process philosophy? Shall it be what is common to Bergson, William James, Peirce, Whitehead, and Mahayana Buddhism? This would be somewhat vague—perhaps the belief that becoming rather than mere being is the basic form of reality. In this statement "reality" must not be taken as a synonym for "being," since we would then have: becoming rather than being is the basic form of being—which hardly makes sense. But real is the contrast term to fictitious (merely feigned or falsely believed) rather than to becoming. The real is independent of any particular experience of it or opinion about it.

That something has become does not make it dependent upon someone's belief in it. Events are as subject to the distinction between real and merely fancied as are things or persons. So the contrast real-unreal has nothing particularly to do with the contrast being-becoming. We do say that things "come into being"; but we thus imply that there is a totality of real things which is subject to *additions*. And this means that the totality referred to by "being," used as synonym for reality, is partly new with each new event or thing.

44

Each moment there is a new whole of real things. Thus being itself and as a whole becomes. But then, since the verbal contrast being-becoming is handy to express the distinction between reality which simply is and reality which comes to be, it is better to stick to "real" for the inclusive term.

Many things come into reality, but not everything does so. Few have thought of God as doing this. Always God is real, he does not have to become real. The mere existence of God is not an instance of becoming, but only of being. For process philosophy, however, the reality of God includes more than his mere existence or being. Rather the divine reality in its concreteness is the eminent form of becoming.

What options are left if we refuse to treat becoming as the basic form of reality? One may hold that being is basic, with becoming a derivative, inferior offshoot, or one may even hold that what is, without becoming, is alone real. Thus dualism or an eternalistic monism. The latter is forced, in spite of itself, to use "real" in two senses. We all have to distinguish the historically real from lies or fancies about what has happened. And there is in addition the suprahistorical which is said to be alone really real. But what genuine analogy is there between the contrast: true versus false history, on the one hand, and historical versus suprahistorical, on the other? One can tell lies or be mistaken about the historical and also about the suprahistorical; but what sense does it make to say that the historical as such is a lie or a mistake? I have read a goodly number of Vedantist essays attempting to throw light upon this question, but I remain in darkness still. As a dream is to waking life so (says the Vedantist) is waking life to the undifferentiated Reality devoid of becoming. But a dream simply as an event or occurrence is just as real as a moment of waking life. Also like the latter it reveals a certain bodily state, at least for anyone with sufficient grasp of the mind-body relationship. The only difference is that certain opinions or meanings which the dreamer himself entertains about his physical state are mistaken in ways in which his waking opinions or interpretations would not be. But the bodily state is always there and colors the dream in many quite direct ways. Moreover, what hint is there in the difference between dreaming and waking that points to the unreality of becoming as such? I fail to find any such hint. Waking life is no less a matter of becoming than dream life.

In the West, dualism rather than eternalistic monism has been the favorite alternative to process philosophy. Changing things are always becoming and never really are, said Plato—who perhaps also knew better. But what about things which never become, but simply are—how do they differ from things which in part at least become? By being superior? Arithmetical truth does not become in any usual sense. Is it then superior to—or more real than—a man who each moment becomes something partly new? The more abstract an idea is the less does becoming seem relevant to it. Is it more real for that reason? Take change in general, the mere abstraction, change as such. Can this itself change? Perhaps immutable being is but the ultimate product of abstracting from all novelty? Which is superior, a changing being conceiving this abstraction, or the mere abstraction he conceives? The Greeks seem to have been unable to give a lucid answer to this question.

In what sense can becoming be an inferior version of reality? Obviously there are inferior forms of becoming. Degeneration is inferior to growth, loss of value inferior to gain in value. Change has apparently two contrary forms, addition-subtraction; creation-destruction; growth-decay. But the claim of process philosophy (found in Bergson, Peirce, and Whitehead—less clearly in Buddhism) is this: the negative side of these dualities is an illusion resulting from confusing the perspective of being and that of becoming, or from an impure use of the language of events or happenings as opposed to the language of beings or substances. It is beings which decay or are destroyed, not happenings. These can do neither. Try to destroy a past event. How would you go about it? Events are immune to destruction. Try to corrupt or impoverish a past event. All you can do is to tell historical lies. You do nothing to the event. Events, once they have occurred, are absolutes, impassible in the old theological sense.

47

Becoming is not basically addition *and* subtraction, but sheer addition. This is the Bergsonian-Whiteheadian proposition. Whitehead's term creativity puts it best. But Bergson had already said, "Duration is invention or nothing." And Peirce had said, "The past is the sum of accomplished facts." The facts are created, they are not subsequently destroyed, wiped out, but only accumulated.

There is of course an old objection: if a reality or value comes to be, it was previously lacking, and if there is addition, the previous sum was not so great as it might have been. So, even though there be no loss, still, looking back, we see that becoming implies deficiency, an aspect of nonbeing. However, this argument makes sense, as an objection to process philosophy, only if it also makes sense to talk about a greatest possible actuality or value. And how do we know that this does make sense? Perhaps, given any actuality a greater is possible. Is a greatest number possible? And in all respects greatest actuality? No process philosopher admits that a simply maximal reality is a consistent idea. If it is not, the only escape from process is to a form of reality which receives no addition, not because it already has all possible values, but because, like arithmetical truths, it can never be anything but an extreme abstraction, incurably lacking in actual or concrete reality or value.

Let us move on to another question.

Philosophies of being, apart from purely monistic

48

versions, conceived a plurality of individual beings distinguished from one another at least by their spatial locations. Philosophies of process can achieve full clarity only by applying the same principle to space-time, rather than space alone. "There are many entities" then becomes "there are many happenings or events." In both philosophies, those of beings and those of events, the plurality of real entities is different from the geometrical plurality of points or point-instants. The right-hand side of a man is not a man or any individual thing, nor is the right-hand side of an atom, and this general principle applies to happenings. A momentary experience of a man corresponds neither to a point of space nor to a mere instant of time, but to a finite volume of space and a finite lapse of time, in fact somewhat less than a tenth of a second. An individual in the ultimate or most concrete sense is both a spatial quantum and a temporal quantum. Mathematical points or instants are ideal entities, in no one-to-one correspondence to actual entities.

An individual person's conscious life consists then of a sequence of momentary experiences, with certain intrinsic relations to their predecessors. The Buddhists seem to have lacked a clear form of the quantum idea; they also failed to make explicit the internal relations to previous quanta.

It is time to consider some religious bearings of all this.

If events are immune to destruction and are sheer

additions to reality, it follows that the constantly growing, never decreasing sum of realities is radically different
from anything which we human beings can possess in
our own right. A sick or senile old man or woman has
truly lost many values once his or hers. And a dead
person has, it seems, lost everything. Nor will posterity
possess what we have lost. Each of us has had many
experiences, some very beautiful, which we have not
communicated effectively to anyone. Posterity will be
farther and farther from the possession of these. The
constantly growing sum of realities is something which
we may be able to conceive abstractly, but which in its
concreteness is quite inaccessible to us. Each good
moment of life is an additional value in the world; but
the sum of these values, for whom is it a value? If the
sum of good things is not good, how is anything really
good?

But if the sum is a good thing, for whom is it
good? Not, it seems, for us. From a naturalistic, humanis-
tic point of view the moments of life are additions to a
total value which is utterly beyond all human possession.
Long, long ago the Buddhists faced this mysterious situation and drew the conclusion that the meaning of life
is not to be found on the level of conscious thought, but
in some mysterious union with the whole of things, a
union which can be experienced but not conceptualized.
But perhaps after all it can in outline be conceived.

Seen from the merely naturalistic perspective *all*

values are ephemeral. In this observation Buddhism is, I think, simply correct. But there are natural illusions which tend to conceal the truth from most of us most of the time. In childhood one anticipates the joys of the next hour, the next day, the next week. In youth one looks forward to adult achievements and possessions. In early manhood one foresees the greater achievements or possessions of riper manhood. Thus the moments of life seem to us contributions to later moments. But then in late middle age, what is the prospect? Of gradual or rapid decline? Of inescapable death? Or does one think of children, pupils, disciples as inheriting values from one's present activities? But then to what will the moments of life of these persons contribute? And how much of one's own contribution will be left after an indefinitely extended series of generations? Can this be the essential way in which values are added to the sum of achieved goods?

Even the Buddhists were not radical enough here. Their belief in reincarnation seems a kind of generalization of the sort of illusion already discussed. Each moment we make decisions that contribute something to our indefinitely prolonged destiny in future incarnations. But the essential receptacle of all contributions, the ever increasing sum of past events—how does reincarnation help us to conceive that? Buddhism did realize that reincarnation is not the essential answer. That answer it left shrouded in mystery. Perhaps this was wise. Still, our theistic tradition does suggest a more positive conception. If the divine consciousness is conceived not as eternally the same, but as perpetually growing in content by virtue of additions from the world, each addition being strictly permanent, once for all, then the ever growing sum of realities and goods can be real and good for someone, for one personal consciousness. From this consciousness, the process version of omniscience, nothing is ever subtracted, but to it all novelties are added. So far, then, from no value being permanent, all values are permanent. But they are permanent not as human but as divine possessions. They are ours only so far as we take as our inclusive aim the divine self-fulfillment. Like Moses who could see the promised land he would never enter, we can foresee the everlasting divine possession of the goods we manage to actualize in ourselves and in the lives of other creatures. In imaginative foresight God's everlasting possession is also ours, but in no other way. In this one way the escape from transience is ours now. The kingdom of Heaven is in this sense present, not future.

In the long run—so I believe—we are nothing, except as God inherits reality and value from our lives and actions. In ultimate perspective all life other than divine is purely contributory. We serve God is the last word, not, God serves us. And our reward? Our reward for serving God is simply that service itself. The essential reward of virtue, as was said long ago, is intrinsic and present, not extrinsic or future. Eventual future gains are for God, not for creatures.

Is this a hard saying? Well, let it never be forgotten that the ancient Jews served God without asking for rewards, at least rewards beyond death. The Devil asked concerning Job, "Does he serve God for naught?" (Or in other words, is he merely seeking rewards?) The climax of the sublime Old Testament book makes no mention of rewards, or of punishments either. Job is shown that he has failed to understand the relation of the cosmic creator or ruler to the ruled or the creatures. He comes to realize that the human concept of omnipotence is inadequate to express this relation. Therefore, the so-called problem of divine justice is not a legitimate one. Process philosophy regards the conventional notion of omnipotence as a pseudoconcept, lacking in any clear and consistent meaning. Before asking *why* God does this or that, we should ask, "What does it mean to say 'God does' something?" The mystery resides not simply in the combination of power and goodness in God but is already present in the notion of divine power just in itself; for this notion is so radically different from ordinary ideas of power that there is no need to introduce the question of divine goodness to sense the limitations of human insight. If evils come to a man, they come from other creatures, not at least directly from God. Other men, other animals, insects, microscopic organisms, atoms

53

—these are the immediate agents of disaster. How is divine agency to be fitted into this?

Job came to see that he had no idea of an answer. So he is able to dismiss the supposed problem of divine justice as pure pretentiousness on the part of man. But the basic question of the Book of Job was not divine justice anyway, but human disinterestedness: can man serve God from mere love of him? The voice from the whirlwind is scrupulously careful not to impugn Job's disinterestedness. He is not threatened, he is not bribed, there is no hint that misfortunes are punishment. Simply he is shown that his grieved perplexity, his sense that God has, as it were, mistreated or misjudged him, rests upon a foolish notion of divine power. To mistreat is at least to treat, to act upon—what understanding can we have of action by a strictly cosmic or supercosmic agent?

The problem comes to this: how can God do everything unless the creatures do nothing? And if the creatures do nothing, what does our word "do," as a word in ordinary use, express? If the word has an ordinary meaning because the creatures are real agents, it is absurd to attribute all that happens to divine agency. Evils may all be attributable to the decisions of creatures —meaning creatures in general, not simply human creatures. The concrete course of events is then not determined by divine decision, or any other one sort of decision, but by the interplay of countless decisions of various kinds. Divine decisions set rules for the game of creaturely interaction, but the rules allow countless options of detail.

If the course of events is not determined by any agent but by the coincidence of the actions of many agents, there is no theological sense in asking why things happen as they do. God's function is not to allocate fortune and misfortune to each of us. It is other creatures who do that, necessarily in large part without knowing what they are doing. God's *initial* function is to enforce rules for the game of life (the laws of nature) but the details of creaturely living are the business of creatures. God's *ultimate* function is to enable the passing moment to have abiding significance, not because we will forever continue to look back upon that moment and profit from it, but because God will do so.

Is it asking too much of people that they should be satisfied to enjoy the beauty of the passing moment and in principle consign to others, ultimately to God, the permanent possession of that beauty?

Here is where the analysis into unit happenings or temporal quanta is relevant to ethics and religion. The philosopher of process views as the final units of reality, not persons or enduring substances, but momentary states or experiences. Concretely I am a new reality each fraction of a second. Each time I say "I" the word refers to a new concrete reality. From a more or less abstract point of view the same reality, the very same person, is denoted: but is not all actual value in the concrete—the momentary states, rather than the ever identical person? If I, as I am now, feel a concern for myself as I may be a year from now, this is a kind of sympathy felt by one unit of actuality for potential future units belonging to the same personal series. But, by very similar bonds of sympathy, I as I am now can feel a concern for potential future units belonging to other personal series. Similarly, if I tend to sympathize with my own past experiences, I can also in a not widely different way sympathize with past experiences of other persons.

In process philosophy all this is quite intelligible. In substance philosophies it is a monstrous paradox. I love myself—of course, says the substance theorist, for I simply am myself—but if I love you, it is across a metaphysical gulf—for I am simply not you. Absolute identity, absolute nonidentity, what light does this schema throw upon the obvious similarities between self-sympathy and sympathy for others? The absoluteness is out of place in both cases. Rather we have relative self-identity and self-love and similarly relative nonidentity and love of others. In some ways I am not myself two seconds running, and in some ways I am my neighbor. My recollections and his often largely overlap, our purposes, hopes, and fears likewise: and as Royce so eloquently argued, what is the self apart from its fund of recollections, and its hopes, aims, and fear for the future? On this issue Whitehead and the Buddhists agree profoundly, whether by coincidence or partly thanks to an influence of Buddhism upon Whitehead I do not know. In either case, the extent of agreement is remarkable. Not another famous philosopher in all the Western tradition has so clearly seen the point. And this includes Schopenhauer, in some ways so close to Buddhism. (I have read three Western writers besides Whitehead who did see the point, but they were not technical philosophers.) For Buddhism as well as for Whitehead the subordination of self-identity to the all-inclusive unity of reality in space as well as in time has ethical and spiritual significance.

One of the three writers just referred to (a South African named S. M. Whiteman) argued that the Jewish-Christian injunction "love your neighbor as yourself," implies the Buddhistic position. And indeed, is it not either stupidity or hypocrisy to say, I am to love my neighbor *as* I love myself, but I view my love for myself as a relation of simple identity and my love for my neighbor as a relation of simple nonidentity? Thus two things are said to be ideally the same and yet in metaphysical truth completely opposite. Read the great Western theologians and metaphysicians of the past, and you will find that one and all are more or less confused and unconvincing on just this question.

Let us consider another topic.

Process philosophy as I conceive it is a philosophy of creativity in a sense which implies limits to causal order. I have little interest in a philosophy of becoming which affirms a strict determinism. Spinoza is the supreme philosopher of determinism; he understood what this doctrine amounts to metaphysically. And unwittingly he showed its inability to make sense out of becoming—or out of anything else.

The idea of creativity has ethical and religious bearings. God is supremely creative. We in our humble way are also creators. How indeed could we have an idea of divine or eminent creativity, if we had no sort of creativity ourselves? From zero one cannot find the way to infinity any more than one can learn what water is by examining some absolutely dry substance. When Jonathan Edwards argued that unless we give absolute sway to causal determination in interpreting our own choices, we lose the right to posit God as supreme "cause," he cut the branch on which alone a theist can stand. For, if choice as we know it is the same as psychological causal necessity, then divine choices as we can conceive them must be necessitated too, so that either Edwards was a Spinozist who concealed his true belief, or else he was badly confused.

Besides, to infer God from the world is to infer cause from effect whereas the *relative* indeterminist (there are no absolute indeterminists, however much determinists like to refute each nonexistent thinkers), the relative indeterminist denies only the converse inferability of effect from cause. By no logical rule known

58

to me can one convert "p entails q" to "q entails p." Odd how often this simple logical truism is forgotten!

We shall assume, then, that process philosophy is not deterministic, presumably even less so than post-Einsteinian physics. It is, however, a rather poor use to make of the indeterminism quantum physics to proclaim proudly that moral responsibility has at last been vindicated against its apparent denial by scientific determinism. Even determinists usually manage to persuade themselves that they can preserve moral responsibility. What they cannot do is to form an intelligible conception of God as creator with the creature as lesser creators cooperating with God. Spinoza said that man is "the absolute slave" of God. Brave honest man! For that is what his philosophy came to. He might have added that God too was a slave, slave of his own eternal, necessary, immutable essence. He does not create, he just is. And what is he? There are but two possibilities: an absolute maximum, all possible concrete values all actual, a formula which there is every reason to think is nonsensical; or else an empty abstraction like the multiplication table. That too is eternally what it is, without the possibility of being anything else or of creating anything additional to itself.

If God truly creates, enriches reality with genuine additions not present or causally implicated in his eternal essence, and if we too can do this, though in a humble, local, more or less blind and faltering way, rather than

59

cosmically and with infallible wisdom, is there not a certain inspiration in this conception? As Bergson has it, we are all "artists," at each moment enriching reality with something not previously there. What we create is primarily, and first of all, our own experiences, each of which is a more or less harmonious, beautiful, and, in its final concrete quality, free response to the myriad stimuli and memories playing upon us at the moment. Indirectly, those experiences contribute to those of other creatures, and finally all contribute to God.

Berdyaev eloquently exalts the imperative: Be creative and foster creativity in others. Rightly he complains that far too little has been said in Christian preaching and moralizing about the contributions of artists, scientists, and other culturally creative people to the life of mankind. All too often the message has been, Obey the basic moral rules (which are chiefly negative) and you will be a sufficiently righteous man and acceptable child of God. It is indeed important not to steal, murder, or falsely defame others. But these are minimal conditions of serving God. Beyond these we should be creative in our little spheres and in our little life-span, as God is creative in his unlimited sphere and forever. Be everywhere and always seeking ways to bring new values to life, that is the true *imitatio dei*. Howard Thurman, a great preacher, educated in Chicago, who happens to be a Negro, once gave an explication of the text, "All things work together for good to them that love God" the following: "It must always be possible to work creatively in any situation."

How many marriages might perhaps be saved if people realized that it is not enough just to persevere in a line once taken, even if the line be no bad one. One needs to be born anew each morning. One needs to hit upon pleasant surprises for others; unpleasant ones are all too sure to occur. Even just being creative of amusement, with pleasantly absurd exaggerations, or other humorous touches, can sometimes be a form of kindness more efficacious than solemn offerings of help. True, such things as humor are partly a gift and all cannot equally excel in them. But many, I suspect, have never thought of it as their religious vocation to make the most of the talents they have for the creation of beauty, humor, delight, as well as righteousness and sobriety in themselves and others. That is why we should take the trouble to read books with some intensity, originality, contagious creativity, rather than those with feebler or more mediocre values.

Innumerable parents take their role to be that of rulers securing obedience by sufficiently severe penalties for violations. They may fancy that that is how God rules the cosmos. Alas, theologians have sometimes encouraged them to think this. They are quite wrong, in my opinion. Job was given no hint from the whirlwind that God is maintaining the cosmos by "sanctions," by inflicting sufferings upon the wayward. Aristotle was in this respect a nobler theologian than many a bishop. God's power over the world, he said, is that "of the beloved over the lover." What does this mean? A great scholar, Chung-Hwan Chen, interprets Aristotle as taking his cue from Plato's dialogue on love, according to which love seeks "absolute beauty." Generalizing this for the universe, Aristotle is saying that it is by his supreme beauty that God moves or inspires the world. He charms it into trying to imitate, as best it can, his own excellence. Whitehead calls this the divine "persuasion," and attributes it to Plato rather than Aristotle. In such a doctrine there is nothing about sanctions.

The ideal parent, whatever else he or she does, charms children into moral and spiritual growth, making constructive actions seem beautiful and delightful in as many ways as possible. From earliest infancy the child, ideally speaking, comes to see in the parents the goodness of life, its joy and ever new aspects of beauty. Given this, perhaps punishment might accomplish something useful now and then; without this, punishment will make a bad matter worse. A mass murderer of recent times had a severe disciplinary father, by the latter's own confession. Probably he does not know even yet how much this may have contributed to the final result. It may well be that the biblical text, wrongly translated I hope, about "sparing the rod and spoiling the child" has spoiled far more children than it has saved. Create values and make the creation of values seem attractive and the failure to create them repulsive: that is how to avoid spoiling children.

I have said almost nothing about Christianity. I shall add a few words about the advantages of the religion of Jesus compared to some others in respect to the philosophy of creativity. Unless the New and Old Testaments are read with an overwhelming bias derived from Greek philosophy, they will give only minor encouragement to the exaltation of being over becoming. In the main, at least, the biblical God is a creator appealing to us as lesser creative agents to make the most of our capacities to add new values to the world. The Bible does not greatly emphasize individual rewards, especially not posthumous ones. It does expressly tell us to value our neighbor *as* we value ourselves, not in some quite different way. It does not, on the whole, imply that life as we know it between birth and death is some kind of great mistake or doom from which we should seek exit. It does not confuse issues, as Hindu Scriptures sometimes do, by telling us we can simply *be,* or we already simply are, the supreme reality, whether the supreme creativity or the supreme reality allegedly beyond creativity. By contrast Judaism, Islam, and Zoroastrianism have, in these respects, somewhat similar merits, and so in a way has Confucianism. But Hinduism and Buddhism must be interpreted in a fairly radically unorthodox way, it seems to me, if they are to rival Christianity as religions of creative process. It can perhaps be done; but it is a privilege, I feel, not to have to do so much reinterpreting.

No doubt there are strands in the Christian tradition which are unhelpful, from the point of view I have been expounding. An example: a defender of what I call Classical Theism, which identifies God with the Uncaused Cause, has put the question to me, "Is not a benevolent divine tyrant preferable to cosmic democracy if the tyrant really is wholly benevolent and wise?" My answer is: "No, if the tyrant is to make our decisions down to the last detail." No benevolence will suffice unless it includes respect for the freedom of others to make their own decisions, to be creators, each in his own proper sphere. Yet whatever difficulties one has with the tradition which comes down from Israel, the correctives for these difficulties seem always to be available in that tradition if one looks for them. The Socinians four centuries ago explicitly conceived human beings as making genuine decisions of their own to such an extent that God himself acquires novel content as these decisions are made. Thus God is not pure being, there is a divine form of becoming. The divine eternity was defined in this tradition not as immutability but as noncontingency with respect to existence. God exists eternally means that he could not *not* exist; it does not mean that he exists always in the same state, incapable of additional values. I have argued at length that it is precisely the philosophy of process which can defend the divine

64

noncontingency or eternity against otherwise fatal objections.

I close with some remarks about the unique symbol of the cross. If deity is a process and not a mere stasis, then the old objections to the idea of a suffering deity become less impressive. Here too, Berdyaev is a clearer guide than Tillich, with all the merits of the latter. Berdyaev unequivocally defends the idea of divine sympathy for the creatures in their sufferings. God is spectator of all existence, but a sympathetic spectator who in some real sense shares in the sufferings he beholds. He is neither simply neutral to these sufferings nor does he sadistically will them for beings outside himself. He takes them into his own life and derives whatever value possible from them, but without ever wanting them to occur. Why then do they occur? As I have already said, because creatures are doing things to one another, not always fortunate things. How could they always be fortunate? The creatures are not infinitely wise or good, as God is, and it is they and not God who finally decide the details of the world's happenings. How could it be otherwise? And even apart from their lack of wisdom or good will, the creatures cannot entirely foresee the way their own decisions will interact with the decisions of others. Not even God can do that, and this not from weakness or deficiency, but simply because really creative decisions are not foreseeable.

Life is process, divinity itself is process, nothing matters but the kinds of processes which occur or can be made to occur. Even the Buddhist's achievement of enlightenment is a process. And all process brings new value into existence. The novelty may be trivial when it could be significant; it may, alas, mean for man the loss of much greater values. But for reality as a whole every new happening is a gain. Our role is to do what we can to maximize this gain. That is all we can do, but it is enough. The ultimate issue, the permanence of values once created, is out of our hands, and in God's forevermore.

3 | Quentin Lauer, S.J. | Phenomenology as Resource for Christian Thinking

Since the title of this lecture points to a somewhat new way of relating philosophical thought and Christian religion, it might be well at the outset to reflect a bit on its meaning. To begin with, I take "resource for Christian thinking" to mean "that to which the Christian can go for significant intellectual support of his religious commitment." Since, however, "phenomenology" is primarily an instrument of *philosophical* methodology, it scarcely seems reasonable to expect from it direct support of a specifically religious commitment. A philosophical methodology cannot enter directly into religious commitment at all. Quite obviously, for example, the Christian cannot put this sort of thing on a level with revelation, which supplies both content and motivation for his faith. Nor can a philosophical method be equated with the ministry of the Word, which makes available to mind and heart the content of revelation. There can, furthermore, be no question of comparing it with grace whose function is to fortify the Christian's subjective response to the object of his faith, nor is it to be counted along with prayer and worship which implement and elaborate this response. By the same token it can in no way be placed alongside the sacraments which embody concretely the grace whereby the Christian lives, prays, worships. Finally it must be said, though some might want to dispute this, that phenomenology cannot be looked upon as strictly speaking contributing to the methodology of the Christian's theology, which on the one hand interprets for him the very meaning of revelation and, on the other, exercises control over the ministry of the Word. If, then, phenomenology is to have significance for Christian thinking, it must be by way of the help it can give to the sort of reflection on religion which we can call a Christian philosophy of religion (or, perhaps, a philosophy of Christian religion).

Having said this, however, we are forced back to an even more fundamental question as to just what a philosophy of religion can be. That it is neither religion nor a substitute for religion, all, I think, will agree. Religion is not and must not become philosophical thinking. It must not, therefore, and cannot be an intellectualizing of genuine religious commitment—that would be a denaturing of religion. Nor is philosophy of religion to be looked upon as a rational reflection on the content of faith, as though, so to speak, religion had to stand trial before the bar of reason before it could legitimately make claims on the believer. It may be that religion must seek to speak a language which reason can in some sense understand, and it may be philosophy's task to elaborate the vocabulary for this; religion itself, however, cannot

68

thereby be rationalized. Furthermore, that of which we speak is not a psychology of religion (however legitimate such a form of investigation may prove to be), whose function is to study what one does when one believes—or, better still, when one responds to the divine initiative. To conclude what may seem a rather negative analysis, there are two other sometime claimants to the title "philosophy of religion," both of which must be rejected. It is not a so-called natural theology, which can be understood either as a *fides quaerens intellectum,* or as an attempt to elaborate rationally a content which turns out to be more or less parallel to the content of belief. Nor is it what I should simply call "Christian philosophy," namely, a philosophical reflection which has its roots in faith as well as in reason and which seeks to reconcile the two where they seem to oppose each other.

If we are to be more positive and to say what a philosophy of religion is, rather than what it is not, we must, I think, begin by approaching the question historically. It is no accident that philosophy of religion, as a legitimate philosophical discipline, appears only in modern times—only, in fact, at the end of the eighteenth or the beginning of the nineteenth century. So long as man's philosophical concern was exclusively the objective content of what was presented to his mind, there was no room for it (although the incomparable religious and philosophical genius of Augustine was far ahead of its time in refusing to look at any truth in isolation from

its significance for man's life). The general picture
changed, when on the religious level Luther turned
men's attention to the subjective assurance of redemption and when, on the philosophical level, Descartes directed attention to the very act of knowing, in an attempt
to establish its validity. Neither Luther nor Descartes,
nor any of the followers of either, it is true, ever sought
to turn the light of philosophical reflection on religion
itself, but they did set the stage for a blending of the two
which had previously not been indicated.

It was not, in fact, until two and a half centuries
later, with the advent of Immanuel Kant, that a way was
opened up for philosophers to examine the religious response as one which was specifically different from that
of rational knowing, ethical judging, or aesthetic contemplation. After Kant the floodgates were open, and
out poured a torrent of "philosophies of religion." We
need cite but a few great names in order to see how their
basic philosophical orientation caused them to disagree in
interpreting religion and the religious act. Fichte, taking
his cue from Kant, saw the religious act as essentially
moral and the God to whom this act was directed as the
"moral order of the universe." For Schelling, who has
been called an "aesthetic pantheist," to find beauty,
whether in nature or in art, was to find God; the religious
and the aesthetic act became inextricably bound up with
each other—if not identified. Schleiermacher sought to
rescue the religious act by establishing its uniqueness.

As a "God-consciousness," which was simultaneously self-consciousness, he distinguished it sharply from any other form of human conciousness, particularly from moral, political, or aesthetic consciousness. For Hegel religion became a relationship to the Absolute, whose medium was image or representation, and which was to be superseded by philosophy's grasp of the Absolute in thought. For the Romantics, of whom Kierkegaard is but the best known and, so to speak, the coping stone, religion was a subjective, emotional attitude, whose validity was somehow independent of the object to which it was directed—though not independent of its own interior divine source.

Against a background such as this the kind of "transcendental phenomenological analysis" which Edmund Husserl espoused inaugurated a new phase in philosophical reflection on the religious act or attitude (though Husserl himself manifested no interest in this aspect of phenomenological investigation). There are several aspects of this sort of investigation which, in the eyes of those phenomenologists who pursue it, recommend it as a method of getting at the very "essence" of the religious attitude. Although phenomenology's concern is with experience and not with the reality of what is experienced, it nevertheless looks not merely to the subjective activity of experiencing but also to the objective content which is inseparable from it, and which, in a certain sense, defines it. Phenomenology asks, then, just what an experience, or type of experience, can reveal regarding its object. If it is true that religious experience is a unique form of experience phenomenology will examine it by itself to see what it reveals both regarding itself and regarding the sort of object which is susceptible of grasp by this and only this sort of experience.

Although William James's *Varieties of Religious Experience* is by no means consciously phenomenological in its methodology, the type of experience James does investigate is eminently susceptible of phenomenological analysis and interpretation. The fact that James's point of view was primarily psychological, and that from this point of view he concerns himself primarily with the experiences as such and with the types of persons who do the experiencing, does not change this at all. If, however, we look for extensive investigations in this area, which are at the same time consciously phenomenological in the Husserlian sense, we must go to the works of Max Scheler,[1] although there is considerable inspiration of this sort too in the brilliant pioneer work of Rudolf Otto,[2] Jean Hering,[3] and G. Van der Leeuw.[4] Without

[1] Chiefly in his *Vom Ewigen im Menschen.* Engl. trans., *On the Eternal in Man,* by Bernard Noble (New York: Harper, 1961).

[2] *Das Heilige.* Engl. trans., *The Idea of the Holy,* by J. W. Harvey (New York: Oxford University Press, 1950).

[3] *Phénoménologie et philosophie religieuse* (Paris: Alcan, 1926).

[4] *Phänomenologie der Religion.* Engl. trans., *Religion in Essence and Manifestation,* by J. E. Turner (London: Allen & Unwin, 1938; Harper Torchbook, 2 vols., 1963).

drawing directly on the work of any of these men, however, I should like to present some reflections on the significance which this sort of phenomenology can have for an understanding of religion in general and of the Christian religion in particular.

THE MEANING OF PHENOMENOLOGY

What, then, is phenomenology? To put it as briefly and as nontechnically as possible, it consists in a methodic examination and analysis of human acts of consciousness, with a view to determining just what is characteristic of a certain type of act and to discovering what the acts investigated reveal regarding their object. It should be remarked here that cognitive acts are not the only acts of consciousness which can be investigated; the emotions, for example, are acts of consciousness; they can be distinguished from one another, and as a result of this they can be seen to have definitely distinct types of object. A well-known example of this sort of thing is the distinction which is made in contemporary "existentialist" literature between the emotions of fear and dread and between the sort of objects which correspond to them. On a large scale this kind of investigation has been carried on with considerable success in a number of areas: perception (Maurice Merleau-Ponty), imagination (Jean-Paul Sartre), will (Paul Ricoeur), hope

73

(Gabriel Marcel), aesthetic response (Georg Simmel), artistic creativity (André Malraux), rational consciousness (Edmund Husserl), social consciousness (Edith Stein), moral consciousness (Dietrich von Hildebrand), religious consciousness (Max Scheler). This does not mean that in each case the method is exactly the same; above all it does not mean that the fundamental attitudes of individual phenomenologists are the same. Some are realists, others are idealists; some are consciously non-metaphysical in their orientation, others are definitively metaphysical; some confine themselves strictly to the phenomenological methodology, others institute a much broader investigation of experience which is only vaguely phenomenological in character. Although what is examined is always some form of consciousness, the goal of the investigation may be to characterize not consciousness but the diverse objects of consciousness. Thus, inquiries of this kind have concerned themselves with consciousness of time or of space, consciousness of self or of other subjects, consciousness of reality, of God—in short of whatever "appears" to man when he thinks, feels, loves, remembers, anticipates, etc.

The most detailed methodology for this sort of investigation was elaborated by Edmund Husserl in a lifetime of meditating chiefly on the method itself. Although not all who draw their inspiration from Husserl accept the whole of his methodology (to say nothing of his presuppositions and conclusions), there are certain common elements discoverable in what has come to be called simply "phenomenology." The most important of these common elements, it would seem, is the insistence on the "intentional" character of every act of consciousness. According to this, not only is all consciousness necessarily consciousness of something, but also that of which it is consciousness is integral to and inseparable from the act itself. One cannot, for example, investigate an act of perceiving without investigating what is perceived, nor can one characterize the activity of perceiving without at the same time characterizing perceived objects. There is also common agreement that phenomenological investigation must confine itself to what is "given" in an act of consciousness, rejecting what is merely assumed to be given, as a result of habit, predisposition, prejudice, etc. This, then, requires some technique of purification, whereby can be eliminated extraneous accumulations which may obscure the act itself and hence its object. If, for example, the act of perceiving contains elements of imagining, it will not be purely an act of perception, nor will its object be only that which is perceived. A third common element is the recognition that the process of past experiences (the history of experience) will condition the very manner of experiencing— that experience, therefore, is always an ongoing process.

The next question, of course, is: can all this be applied to an investigation of religious consciousness? (The question of what the investigation will discover we can leave to later.) The answer to the question will be, yes, if religion fulfills three requirements. (1) Religion must be a unique manner of experiencing, which is not reducible to other forms of consciousness, such as moral consciousness, rational consciousness, feeling, projection of needs, etc. (2) The object of religious consciousness must not be susceptible of grasp by any other form of consciousness. (3) There must be a clear-cut sphere of religious acts, which can be purified of extraneous elements and then analyzed as such. It is the contention of those who engage in the "phenomenology of religion" that all these conditions are fulfilled in religious consciousness and that an investigation of this kind can make the religious man more aware of the nature of his own commitment. It should, of course, be remarked that this does not mean that such a phenomenology will make anyone more religious. Consisting as it does in a reflection on an already existent religious commitment, it is not itself religious, though its motivation may well be religious. The contention is, however, that philosophical reflection (in this case phenomenological) can make the religious act more meaningful, just as philosophical reflection on any experience can reveal more and more meaning in the experience itself—can in fact condition the form of subsequent experience.

There is another aspect of this question which is by no means unimportant, if our study is to result in more than merely methodological considerations. If all one's experiences are colored by previous experiences, then religious experience will color the way one experiences oneself, other men, and the world in which we all live; and the religious experience will in turn be colored by the sum total of one's other experiences. We cannot, nor should we try to, recapture the religious experiences of the past, be they our own or those of other men, no more than we can or should try to recapture the political, social, or scientific experiences of ancient Greece, the Middle Ages, or colonial America. Not only man has a history, so does his experience; it is ever moving, ever growing; and religious experience is no exception to this. This means, of course, that no experience is without religious significance, but it also means that religion is constantly significant for the totality of experience. The religious and the nonreligious man simply do not see things in the same way.

Let us take an example. In recent years the writings of Pierre Teilhard de Chardin have been attracting a great deal of attention and creating a significant stir throughout the world. He is idolized by many, not only outside of, but to some extent, at least, within the scientific community. There exists, however, a hard core of scientists or scientific philosophers who find that his work outside his own field of scientific specialization (paleontology) pretends to be but is not scientific. Much of this criticism is due to his own designation of his *Phenomenon of Man*[5] as a "mémoire scientifique," which in the unfortunate English translation of the work has been rendered as a "scientific treatise," which it is not and does not pretend to be. What this work—and many of his other writings—does contain, however, are a scientist's reflections on much that his science suggests but does not, strictly speaking, prove. These reflections on man, the world, and God would not have been possible, if Teilhard had not been a scientist, if he had not accumulated vast stores of scientific knowledge and experience which permitted him to see what others simply did not see. The reflections, however, would have been equally impossible, if Teilhard had been only a scientist, if he had not been in addition a philosopher and a man of strong religious faith. His religious experience gave another dimension of meaning to his scientific experience, just as the latter gave constantly new dimensions of meaning to his Christian faith. The result was a religious commitment which, though remarkably open to the realities of scientific and technical progress, did not thereby lose anything of the depth which his faith gave it. By the same token his scientific work became characterized by what can only be called a religious reverence

[5] Pierre Teilhard de Chardin, *Le phénomène humain*. Engl. trans., *The Phenomenon of Man*, by Bernard Wall (New York: Harper, 1959; Harper Torchbook, 1961).

78

before the world, nature, material reality, and man's progressive conquest of the forces surrounding him.

PHENOMENOLOGY OF RELIGION

Having come this far, it now seems that we can turn to some reflections on what in the concrete a phenomenology of religion would mean. It should be pointed out at the outset, however, that such a method of investigation would not be theologically concerned with the objective truth or falsity of religious ideas, only with what can be said about religion and about God as the result of a consideration of authentically religious experience. It should also be pointed out that, if the investigation is to be genuinely phenomenological, it would seem that it must be carried out by one for whom religious experience is a reality in his own life. One might go so far as to say that it is impossible to investigate phenomenologically an act of devotion, for example, if the object of the act is not a reality for the one investigating. A purely "objective" study of religious acts could scarcely be more than statistical, resulting in some sort of "psychology of religion," which is in truth a study of the religious man but not of religion itself at all.

Given this assumption, then, there is more than one possible point of departure. (1) One could, like James in *Varieties of Religious Experience*, look at what a large number of individuals, at different times and in a

79

wide variety of circumstances, have said about their own religious (or mystical) experiences. This, of course, runs the risk of being somewhat indiscriminate and of ultimately presenting a mere catalogue of responses which are called religious if they manifest a certain set of predetermined characteristics. (2) Another starting point might be the sort of monumental inquiry undertaken by Van der Leeuw in his *Religion in Essence and Manifestation.* Here it is not individuals but religions which are examined. Nor is it merely the characteristics of the subjective response which are determined. There is much more concern for what is being experienced and with the extent to which the experience reveals a sphere of objectivity which is susceptible of penetration only by an activity which is authentically religious—without determining beforehand what this authentically religious activity will be. (3) A third possibility, which presupposes as background the sort of study just mentioned, would be to investigate, as Otto does in *The Idea of the Holy,* a whole sphere of phenomena in which a divine Being is said to reveal himself in and through human experience. Here the general name for the religious phenomenon is "the holy," bespeaking an object which, though given only in the religious act, is seen to have a reality, a power, and a claim on human commitment, which transcend the subjective response in which they are revealed. (4) A fourth type of investigation is of the kind instituted by Scheler, chiefly in his *On the Eternal in Man.*[6] Only this last is a strictly phenomenological investigation in the Husserlian sense (although Scheler disagrees with Husserl on many not unimportant counts). Characteristic of this approach is its attempt to get at the very essence of religious consciousness and correlatively (since, as we have said, consciousness is meaningful only as related to its object) to determine what can be said of the religious object, i.e., God. Because Scheler, unlike Husserl, is a realist and not a transcendental idealist, he is convinced that his type of phenomenological investigation finds in the religious act an infallible indication that its object is the real, living, and true God, not merely what a God would have to be if he did exist.

As different as these four approaches may be, and with the exception of Van der Leeuw's and Otto's they are irreducibly different, they do have common elements, i.e., they are based on certain common convictions: (1) That the paradigm of religious consciousness is to be found in the specially gifted religious person and—with the possible exception of James—that the paradigm of all paradigms is Jesus Christ himself. (2) That it is a mistake to try to understand (a fortiori to judge) religious categories such as revelation, redemption, conversion,

[6] Though the differences in approach are not such that would here warrant a separate treatment, we must not fail to mention—and recommend—the brilliant work of Mircea Eliade in this field. Cf., for example, *The Sacred and the Profane,* trans. from the French by Willard R. Trask (New York: Harper, 1961).

worship, illumination, grace, etc. on the basis of merely rational or scientific criteria—since, as Scheler says, there is an "objective logic of religious thought," [7] which is simply not the logic of merely rational thought, nor is it to be subjected to the criteria of the latter. (3) That it is possible to get behind the obvious varieties of manifestation to something more than a least common denominator of religions and the religious, i.e., to something like an understanding of what is the essentially religious. (4) That reflection on religious experience, which can itself be rational, constantly affirms rather than dissipates the essential ineffability of the God to which religious consciousness is directed. (5) That the nonrational character of the religious response does not forbid rational reflection on it and that the latter in no way runs the risk of rationalizing religion but does in fact make it possible to deepen the experience itself. (6) That the Christian religious consciousness not only will not suffer from but will be illumined and enriched by contact with what is peculiar to the response and the content of the great religions of the world.

THE MEANING OF RELIGION

Without going into the elaborate technicalities of the phenomenological methodology we can, perhaps, in

[7] *On the Eternal in Man,* p. 279.

a tentative sort of way, consider some of the characteristics of religious consciousness which such a methodical investigation *might* reveal. This, I hope, will enable us to return to our original question as to whether it is possible to speak in a meaningful way of phenomenology as a resource for Christian thinking. In so doing we must, of course, remember two limitations which a necessarily generalized discussion cannot overcome. (a) Although there is some justification in seeking to characterize religious response in general, it is still true that the actual responding is done by individuals, and there is something unique about any individual response which simply remains opaque to even the most conscientious and sympathetic investigation. (b) In addition, since the investigation must be carried on by persons and not by machines, it is clear that neither you nor I can engage in such an investigation without bringing with us an already articulated point of view (the Husserlian "presuppositionless" attitude is little more than a dream). This may well result in certain irreducible differences in the way we both see the same phenomena. When the investigation is carried on (or even merely described) without the aid of concomitant dialogue—as it must be when one takes upon himself the responsibility of delivering a lecture—even resolvable differences may loom larger than they have a right to do. With these cautions we may proceed.

Every experience, however insignificant, does something to one's subsequent manner of experiencing. Since, then, no one can approach any phenomenon without a vast background of previous experiences, in every experience more is given than the mere direct object of that experience. Thus it is clear to anyone who has taken the trouble to look seriously at human behavior in both its historical and its worldwide dimensions that it is accompanied almost universally by the consciousness of a being, a force, a presence, which transcends the immediate natural object of any experience or sum total of experiences. It is equally clear that this "transcendent" presence has called forth from men a type of response which, though it be sophisticated in cultured societies and more or less unsophisticated in so-called "primitive" societies, constitutes a sphere of what must be called religious acts, which, though they cannot be rationally justified, cannot at the same time be justifiably rejected on rational grounds. Activities such as those of prayer, reverence, devotion, blessing, piety, worship, and a host of others, can no more be rationally explained than they can be rationally explained away.

Despite epistemological difficulties, dating back to the early Greeks and cropping up again in almost every age since then, it has always been impossible to convince the ordinary man—and even the philosopher when he is not philosophizing—that his direct experiences do not deliver to him real objects in a real world. By the same token the efforts of naturalistic skeptics have done little to shake man's confidence in his religious experience and in the reality of the object it makes available to him. It is possible, nevertheless, to examine that experience more closely, not for the purpose of discrediting it but rather in order to realize more adequately just what it does reveal. The answer to such an inquiry is paradoxical: this sort of experience reveals a being which is beyond experience, beyond thought, beyond man's capacities of expression, a presence which asserts itself with a force that is in inverse proportion to man's capacity to conceptualize what he is experiencing. Martin Heidegger says of Being that the more it reveals itself the clearer it becomes that it is hiding itself in so doing. The same can be said of the God who reveals himself in and through religious experience; the more thoroughly the experience comes to grips with him, the clearer it becomes that he is an essentially hidden God; the closer one comes to the object of this experience, the more clearly God reveals that he is not an object at all but a subject who can be encountered, can be spoken to, can, if you want, be wrestled with, but cannot be objectified. When we plunge into the mystery of God, the mystery is not cleared up; it simply becomes clearer to us that he is mysterious—and the paradox of this is that precisely this brings us closer to him. When we say of God that he is mysterious, hidden, ineffable, we are not throwing up our hands in despair; we are drawing closer to him; we are learning that in proportion as our capacity to speak *about* him decreases, our capacity to speak *to* him increases. To paraphrase Leslie Dewart, we do not seek more ways to name God, we seek more ways of speaking to him without naming him at all.[8]

If we move from this basic God-consciousness to the specifically Christian consciousness of Jesus Christ as God and Savior, the paradox becomes even more manifest (more manifestly paradoxical). As Kierkegaard has so masterfully pointed out, it is in and through history that we become acquainted with Jesus Christ, and yet history is powerless to reveal to us just what Jesus Christ really is. What is it, then, which does reveal this to us? It is faith, to be sure, but faith is no more a merely subjective, emotional response to a we-know-not-what, than it is an intellectual response to what has been rationally established. Faith is a heightened capacity to grasp and respond to a real presence which is unavailable to reason. It carries with it a realization that the capacity to believe does not spring from our own natural talents and effort but is the result of a divine condescension. The activity of believing is our own; it has its roots, however, in an initiative which we recognize as more than our own.

[8] *The Future of Belief* (New York: Herder & Herder, 1966), p. 214.

In line with what has already been said it becomes possible with the help of just such a phenomenological investigation to recognize that, without religion, a dimension of man's being is missing. The religious response can be seen as fundamental to the overall human structure of response —even its substitutes illumine this—and without religion man is seen (in contradiction of the Marxist's contrary assertion) as "alienated" from his authentically human orientation. One can, of course, be a pessimist and say that this orientation is meaningless, since man is condemned to the perpetual frustration of his most fundamental exigencies. But, if we refuse pessimism—and the refusal is a choice—we cannot fail to see that no finite reality can ever satisfy those very same exigencies. As Scheler very succinctly puts it:

Only a real being with the essential character of divinity can be the cause of man's religious propensity, that is, the propensity to execute in a real sense acts of that class whose acts, though finite experience cannot fulfill them, nevertheless demand fulfillment. The *object* of religious acts is at the same time the *cause* of their existence. In other words, all knowledge of God is necessarily knowledge from God.[9]

Although this is neither the time nor the place to settle all controverted questions regarding religious

---

[9] *On the Eternal in Man*, p. 261.

activity, it does seem that the sort of phenomenological investigation I have been describing (however vaguely) does provide a viable approach to just such issues. According to Schleiermacher, for example, although authentic religion will not fail to be accompanied by moral integrity, religion itself is entirely distinct from and independent of moral consciousness. I suggest that a phenomenological inquiry into the very God-consciousness of which Schleiermacher speaks might well reveal not only that it is inseparable from moral overtones, but that these moral overtones enter into the very constitution of a properly religious attitude (without, of course, ever reducing religion to the role of a *means* to morality or God to the role of a support for moral activity). A somewhat similar mode of investigation might also reveal that a religious commitment is truncated if it does not express itself in ritual acts, or if it tries to be merely personal and individual, refusing to recognize its own necessarily communal dimensions. Finally, I suggest that a genuine grasp of what makes the religious act to be religious may reveal to us that the pursuit of truth, goodness, beauty, in whatever form it occurs, may have inescapable religious dimensions. In the words of Van der Leeuw:

All understanding, irrespective of whatever object it refers to, is ultimately religious; all significance sooner or later leads to ultimate significance. As Spranger states this: "in so far as it always refers to the whole man, and actually finds its final completion in the totality of world conditions, all understanding has a religious factor. . . . we understand each other in God." [10]

[10] *Religion in Essence and Manifestation*, p. 684.

4 | Frederick Ferré

The Two Faces of Socrates—Language Analysis as Resource for Christian Thought

Concern about accuracy and adequacy in language is as old as philosophy itself. One poignant example is depicted in Plato's account of Socrates' death. In the *Phaedo,* after a long discussion of the grounds for belief in the immortality of one's true self and of the need for care in the cultivation of one's immortal soul, the earthy and loyal disciple Crito makes an apparently innocent remark: "Then," said Crito, "we shall strive to do as you bid us. But how are we to bury you?" [1]

Socrates laughs quietly. After all this discussion Crito has betrayed, in a pronoun, his unchanged belief that Socrates, the *real* "you," is identical with a body. Was it only a slip of the tongue? No excuse! Carelessness in speaking leads to error in thought, and errors of some kinds lead to great distress or even to vice. "My best of friends," Socrates warns Crito good-humoredly, "I would assure you that misuse of language is not only distasteful in itself, but actually harmful to the soul."

This, then, is my text. I approach language analysis

[1] This and the following quotations are taken from Vol. I, *Philosophical Classics: Thales to St. Thomas,* ed. by W. Kaufmann and used by permission.

as a resource for Christian thinking in a Socratic mood. There is nothing exclusive in the position I have come to present; my view of linguistic philosophy is too heedful of its failures, its excesses, and its need for reform along the lines of its own best principles to permit me the partisan satisfaction of equating "philosophy of language" with just plain "philosophy." Likewise, my sense of the reaches of legitimate philosophic activity beyond the normal range of problems dealt with in the linguistic mode makes me slightly uneasy with my own frequent classification among the linguistic analysts. I will not *deny* being a linguistic philosopher if someone cares to give me the label, but I do not seek it. Just earning the title of philosopher would be good enough for me.

But in the end this is all that language analysts really should ask. Analytical philosophy is, I believe, simply a style of engaging in the philosophic enterprise by way of attempting to take the Socratic warning with adequate seriousness. Here I can identify myself without embarrassment. The enterprise of language analysis is the common quest for *understanding the world of meaning* that men inhabit as naturally and inescapably as fish inhabit water. The distinctive style of analytical philosophy, if it is distinctive, is found in the presumption that it is always apt to prove valuable to be alert (early and constantly) to the character of the medium of language that carries, expresses, and shapes thought. The more aware we are of the medium itself, the less likely we are to fall into Crito's distress. The more we know about language, its possibilities and its tricks, the less vulnerable we shall be to intellectual disorientation or distortion by unsuspected currents, refracting layers, or other discontinuities in our conceptual environment. As I commend it to you, therefore, language analysis is more a manner of swimming in the common medium of meaning—cautiously, with eyes wide—than a matter of agreed conclusions. Conclusions may differ rather sharply among us, but the Socratic distaste for misuse of language is a uniting passion.

How, then, can this approach become a resource for Christians? My thesis is that language analysis in its relation with Christian thought wears two masks. Both have the same features—the flat, pug-nosed, helpful features of Socrates—but the effects of the two faces are electrifyingly different.

I

Language analysis wearing the first face of Socrates is described in Plato's *Meno*. In that dialogue the philosopher has been baffling his previously confident young companion by leading him into unsuspected difficulties implicit in defining "virtue." Every attempt has failed him, and now Meno is piqued into some unflattering counterattacks both on Socrates' appearance and his methods.

O Socrates, I used to be told, before I knew you, that you were always doubting yourself and making others doubt; and now you are casting your spells over me, and I am simply getting bewitched and enchanted, and am at my wits' end. And if I may venture to make a jest upon you, you seem both in your appearance and in your power over others to be very like the flat torpedo fish, who torpifies those who come near him and touch him, as you have now torpified me, I think. For my soul and my tongue are really torpid, and I do not know how to answer you; and though I have been delivered of an infinite variety of speeches about virtue before now, and to many persons—and very good ones they were, as I thought—at this moment I cannot even say what virtue is.

Exactly here, in the mask of the Socratic torpedo fish,[2] analytical philosophy has in recent years made its first useful but unpleasant contribution to Christian thought by shocking and shocking again. Let me illustrate the effect of the torpedo's touch on two areas of great importance to Christians: thought about God and thought about Christ.

The language of theological assertion, or purported assertion, has been a problematic focus for Christian thinkers almost as long as there have been Christians; there is nothing especially novel in this area of the torpedo's shock. But the manner of the challenge has

[2] *Malapterurus,* the electric catfish of the Nile.

changed among philosophers impressed by the amazing conceptual successes of the sciences, just as the radical impact on torpified Christian tongues has been greatly heightened by a culture whose common sense has been molded by technological empiricism.

Let us take a central example of Christian theological speech, like "God loves the world." *What does it actually assert?* asks the modern mask of Socrates. One of the ways, it would seem, of understanding such an utterance would be to compare it with similar ones like "Mr. Brown loves his family." I do not want to suggest any naïve identification of these two sentences. God's love would presumably be much greater than any human love could ever be, and it might be manifested in appropriately different ways, but the logic of the utterances *must to some degree be alike:* unless some shared sense were being conveyed, Christians would have no ground for using this language rather than any other. If these sentences have *no* common meaning, Christians have to face the charge of playing fast and loose with empty speech.

But, language analysts have been saying recently to Christian thinkers, look for a moment at the actual logical situation! When we assert that Mr. Brown loves his family we are, in a very general way, making a prediction about specifiable experiences that we should (or should not) anticipate under definable circumstances. If Mr. Brown loves his family, he will (for instance) guard

94

their health—of body and of mind—in every way open to him. If Mr. Brown loves his family, again, he will certainly do everything possible to rescue them from their burning house if it should catch on fire. The "cash value" factual content—i.e., the appropriate empirical information—of the assertion of Mr. Brown's love for his family, we see, is extremely wide. The statement functions as an empirical hypothesis promising a vast range of possibly confirming experience. But we must note that this range is not wide without limit. There are specifiable types of experiences that we may expect *not* ever to have if the hypothesis is meaningful and true. We are aware, for instance, that if Mr. Brown should stand by indifferent to the screams of his trapped and burning family—perfectly able to help (perhaps by unlocking a door) but making no obvious effort to do so—we could conclude that the assertion of his love for them had been horribly falsified. That sort of experience is exactly the sort which, given "Mr. Brown loves his family," we are entitled to dismiss from among our anticipations of the future.

"God loves the world," though, despite its grammatical similarity to "cashable" hypotheses, has traditionally been different in this crucial respect. Think of what has been taken as compatible with its utterance: drought, famine, plague, flood, earthquake, defective babies—all these are somehow nonfalsifying events, though presumably God, traditionally defined, has full

PHILOSOPHICAL RESOURCES FOR CHRISTIAN THOUGHT

competence to prevent them. What empirical conse-
quence does "God's love" involve? The innocent suffer
as badly as the wicked—perhaps even worse, as the
famous jingle laments:

> The rain, they say, falls on the just
> And on the unjust fella;
> But mostly on the just, because
> The unjust has the just's umbrella.

And if this has been the case, then what *could* serve as
a limit to the empirical promiscuousness, the indiscriminate mingling or association with statements of fact,
characteristic of theological claims? If *no* possible expectations are ruled out on the basis of a paradigm sentence
like "God loves the world," and this seems to be the
case, then in good logic it must be concluded that the
sentence is not, despite appearances, functioning as a
factual empirical hypothesis.

The Christian thinker suddenly finds himself in a
dilemma. Either he admits that his language about God
is unfalsifiable by any specifiable set of experiences,
or he refuses to admit this. But he is in difficulties either
way: the first choice seems to impale him on the horn
of empirical emptiness for theistic language; but the
second choice not only challenges his traditional ontological formulations but also trivializes his Christian conviction by threatening to reduce its "cash value" to claims

about observable, finite, and contingent events. Further, if he hopes to avoid these horns, he discovers that the burden is on him to account for the meaning of his language. It is not enough to say that it is "different," or "analogical." This is offering a mere label in place of an explanation. *How* does his language make sense without falling into either obscurantism or triviality?

What does "God loves the world" *mean?* Does it mean anything at all? Do any statements about God have factual meaning? The torpedo shock is at work, and many a Christian thinker may be imagined to say:

O Socrates, . . . now you are casting your spells over me. And though I have delivered an infinite variety of sermons about the "love of God" before now, and to many congregations—and very good ones they were, as I thought—at the moment I cannot even say what, or whether, language about God can assert.

In this state of "torpor" some Christian thinkers have decided to abandon talk about God as a distinct liability. Professor Paul M. van Buren, for example, proposes a shift from what he condemns as factually vacuous language about God to a radically empirical Christian discourse composed of reports of attitudes, historical perspectives, and basic assumptions ("verifiable" in an extended sense, though the types of experience may be private and personal)—all of these informed by basic historical claims about the character of Jesus Christ as a "remarkably free man." As long as it can claim firm empirical footing in history, then, *Christology* may be able to survive in a secular-technical age while *theology* expires. This, at any rate, is one suggestion that language analysis should take seriously.

The best and most thorough application of the methods of analytical philosophy to questions of christological belief and historical judgment is, I think, to be found in Van A. Harvey's new book, *The Historian and the Believer.*[3] I commend those who may be especially interested in this topic to follow for themselves the richness and care of Harvey's own analysis, an analysis to which a brief lecture like this one cannot possibly do justice. But, essentially, Harvey successfully performs the Socratic torpedo-fish function against Christian tendencies to play fast and loose with their language about the "historical Jesus" and the "Christ of faith." Language analysis, as Harvey reminds us, has shown that there exists an enormous variety of functions for language, even language within a single human enterprise. And language analysis has further shown that these different functions have different ways of being supported or justified, depending upon the kind of work they are intended to do. Even statements employed in the same general way, to assert some fact or other, may be of

[3] (New York: The Macmillan Company, 1966.)

quite different types depending upon their role. (Is this statement an inductive generalization, a putative law, a theoretical construct, a singular categorical assertion?) Moreover, statements of the same fact-alleging type may themselves be very different in their right to demand reasonable assent, depending on how weighty or well-knit the complex network of considerations which supports them.

Since this is the case for any field of human interest, Harvey has no difficulty in showing how preeminently true it is for the language of the critical historian. History is a "field-encompassing field," and the kinds of assent appropriate to various historical propositions are most diverse.

What, in light of these logical considerations, becomes of the hope both to hang onto history as a factual, empirical ground for Christian thought and to tie one's ultimate perspectives to the inspiring vision of Jesus' internal life, his "freedom," or the authenticity of his existential selfhood? Harvey couches his criticism of the "new quest" for the historical Jesus—the quest relied upon by would-be empirical thinkers like van Buren— not against the "new questers'" concern for historical fact nor for their admiration of the "free" Christ to whom they commend Christian commitment, but for their confusion of the logical status of different—and differently weighted—assertions. "Heavy" assent may, perhaps, be logically appropriate to language referring to the crucifixion of an obscure person from Nazareth named Joshua or Jesus, and even regarding the probable reactions of the early church to certain vaguely conjecturable events surrounding the life and death of this man; but when it comes to making assertions about the motives, feelings, or choices that constitute the "inner life" of this distant figure, only the most tentative claims are logically in order.

The "inner life" of Abraham Lincoln, as Harvey points out, is still largely a mystery despite the volumes of excellent data, including eyewitness accounts, authentic speeches, and so on, available to historians; even claims about one's own "existential selfhood" may be full of risk, as modern psychology has demonstrated. How much more tentative, therefore, must any claim be, supposing that it genuinely accepts the logic of critical history rather than a priori assumption of nonempirical faith, if it presumes to declare at all the "heart of hearts" of Jesus.

On what *historical* evidence can it be shown that Jesus did not, despite his reported cry of dereliction, lose both faith and freedom before his death? The Christ of perfect wholeness and authenticity, of unmatched freedom and unblemished love, is a fabricated Jesus of faith, of whom critical history can know nothing worth saying. Only by misusing language, by confusing the language of "heavy" historical assent with the language of crucial religious passion, could the inherent fraud seem so plausible and survive so long.

What *can* be said about a Christ worthy of our faith, then, that is not in violation of the morality of critical thinking? The Socratic torpedo shock lends torpor to the tongue of those it touches, and once again we can imagine the Meno-like wail arising from the churches:

O Socrates, . . . though I have delivered an infinite variety of talks about "the Man for others" and "Christ's perfect love" before now, and to many membership classes—and very good ones they were, as I thought—at the moment I cannot even say what historically warranted propositions about a religiously interesting Christ could be.

In these two central examples drawn from Christian language about God and about Christ, I have tried to show how analytical philosophy, wearing the first (not very lovely) face of Socrates—the face of the electric catfish, *Malapterurus*—can serve as helpful resource for Christian thinking.

Helpful? yes, *helpful* in the first and most necessary way that philosophy can be so. Let me illustrate by returning for a moment to the *Meno*. Soon after Socrates has been compared to the numbing torpedo fish, he is engaged in an unusual geometry lesson with Meno's slave boy. The slave boy, in his ignorance, supposes that doubling the side of a square would result in a doubled area. Socrates, instead of simply asserting (as from a vantage point of external wisdom or authority) that the boy is wrong, leads him gradually—by questioning—to see *for himself* the impossibility of this answer. Halfway through this episode the boy acknowledges his ignorance and confusion, whereupon Socrates breaks off to have the following interesting exchange with Meno:

Socrates: He did not know at first, and he does not know now . . . : but then he thought that he knew, and answered confidently as if he knew, and had no difficulty; now he has a difficulty, and neither knows nor fancies that he knows.

Meno: True.

Soc.: Is he not better off in knowing his ignorance?

Meno: I think that he is.

Soc.: If we have made him doubt, and given him the torpedo's shock: have we done him any harm?

Meno: I think not.

Soc.: We have certainly, as it would seem, assisted him in some degree to the discovery of the truth; and now he will wish to remedy his ignorance. . . .

Meno: True.

Soc.: But do you suppose that he would ever have inquired into or learned what he fancied that he knew, though he was really ignorant of it, until he had fallen unto perplexity under the idea that he did not know, and had desired to know?

Meno: I think not, Socrates.

Soc.: Then he was better for the torpedo's touch?

Meno: I think so.

Then Socrates goes on to lure the slave boy and, after that, Meno himself to more adequate ideas on the respective subjects at hand.

The point is too obvious, is it not, for me to labor? If Christian thought has difficulties, Christians are better off aware of these difficulties than in a state of ignorance, however blissful. And if the torpor of tongue that is spread by the touch of language analysis is felt widely and deeply among Christians, so much the more likely, then, that Christian thinkers will be moved to recognize and heed the *second* face of Socrates which may also be worn by philosophers of language.

II

For a description of this second face I turn to Plato's *Symposium*. The setting is a celebration banquet, and all the guests have entertained themselves by speeches in praise of *Eros*. The magnificent next-to-last speech is that of Socrates, who describes *Eros* as the half-divine principle of longing—for the beautiful, or the good and true—which drives and stirs the lover to more and more adequate objects of love: up from the partial to the perfect, up from the fragmentary to the full. But it is significant, I think, that the last speech of all is not *by* Socrates but *about* him, for we suddenly realize, as we listen to the hopelessly enamored Alcibiades, that Socrates himself represents *Eros* in human flesh, the living principle of the pursuit of excellence. Alcibiades, rather the worse for wine, begins:

And now, my boys, I shall praise Socrates in a figure which will appear to him to be a caricature, and yet I speak, not to make fun of him, but only for truth's sake. I say, that he is exactly like the busts of Silenus, which are set up in the statuaries shops, holding pipes and flutes in their mouths; and they are made to open in the middle, and have images of gods inside them. I say also that he is like Marsyas the satyr. You yourself will not deny, Socrates, that your face is like that of a satyr.

The snub-nosed face of a satyr, symbol of erotic pursuit, is the second form, then, in which the philosopher—the relentless lover of wisdom—may be apprehended. And in this mask some philosophers of language, too, hope to lure Christians from infatuation with misleading ways of speaking to fuller and more adequate speech and thought.

Once again I shall have to be content with being simply illustrative. But in terms both of theological and christological speech there is a considerable field for the Socratic pursuit of excellence.

First, there is a call to the *beauty of precision* in meaning. Theological thinking done in dialogue with language analysis is urged, that is, to delight in the chance to become far clearer than ever before about the variety of meanings carried by ordinary Christian discourse. Such speech is woven out of innumerable threads of many textures and many hues. Not just one meaning but several—all interlaced—may be involved in a typical expression like "God loves the world." It may serve to express a sense of joy or confidence in history and in the cosmos; it may evoke relief and release within the suffering or the cynical; it may strengthen one's moral resolve to refrain from hateful acts and attitudes; it may summarize a distinctive sense of existential selfhood; it may function to bind a scattered society into a genuine community. And, of course, most Christians suppose that it may be used to convey a very basic belief, to report on a very important fact. Acknowledging the beauty of precision, recognizing this variety of function, can be important. It helps Christian perspective. It may prevent costly confusion and empty disputes.

But wait. Have we any longer the right to add the last, *belief-asserting* function to our list? The joy in attending to the riches of the tapestry of theological speech fades quickly for many Christians, if they are in the end required to confess that they cannot see how this speech can function to carry belief claims about any states of affairs. All the other functions so lovingly distinguished become pointless, rootless, or even irresponsibly unwise apart from the belief-asserting or cognitive possibility. Socrates himself, besides assisting in making vital distinctions and luring his partners in discourse to increased clarity of meaning, was ever interested in truth. Has truth been put beyond the reach of Christian thought, however, by the previously noted empirical unfalsifiability of theological utterances? These are vital questions indeed! The second theological area, therefore, where we may hope for an effective Socratic lure toward increased adequacy of understanding is in the *pursuit of better accounts* of the truth-alleging functions of theological speech.

If in pursuit of such analysis we want to contemplate, as a model, some of the best work done by language philosophy—work that is highly sensitive to subtlety and variety in cognitive functions—we should look, I believe, to the most recent developments in the philosophy of science. Scientific thought has prompted the best efforts from analytical philosophers because, after all, judged by its fruits it is the best kind of thought we have. When theological or other such forms of thought and speech fail to live up to philosophic expectations, it is a comparatively simple matter to demand that their proponents "like it or lump it." But when *scientific* cognition proves to be too complex for philosphic reconstructions to fit, then it is more likely that philosophers, not scientists, will need to accept the lumps. Once this happens, once new refinements are introduced for the sake of science into the philosophic account of cognition, then perhaps the satyr's flute may dispel some of the torpor from theological tongues as well.

I can only hint here at what, concretely, this may imply. First, it may release the theologian from his painful dilemma of factual vacuousness versus triviality, which we noted earlier. The release will not, however, come from any ingenious attempts to assimilate statements like "God loves the world" to empirical hypotheses like "Mr. Brown loves his family." Crucial theological utterances are simply not falsifiable empirical hypotheses, and it would be a great advance for Christians to learn this lesson as thoroughly and as intimately for themselves as Meno's slave boy learned his.

But awareness of blocked passages is only the first step out of a maze; a more positive clue is found in the relatively recent consensus among language analysts that a variety of scientific assertions are indeed fact-stating and referential but at the same time not reducible to empirical hypotheses. The assertions of scientific *theory*, for example, unlike empirical generalizations, are often far removed from the "ground level" of gross observations and inductive laws that the theory attempts to interpret and explain. A rather different set of considerations are appropriate to the *weighing* of a theory, on the one hand, and the *verification* or *falsification* of an empirical hypothesis, on the other. Perhaps, then (so the Socratic lure may be heard to urge), this might be a better way for Christians to understand the logic of their theological language within its cognitive function: namely, as a very comprehensive kind of *theory*, with a logic at some points similar to scientific theory.

Yes, but by now the course of this little dialogue with analytic philosophy should have strengthened the Christian thinker to a bit more independence of his teacher. (That is, in fact, precisely the hoped-for advantage of dialectic over dogma.) If analyses of "good thinking" were too "crude" before, the Christian may muse, to account for scientific as well as theological thinking, and if they are now being revised to take fuller account of the actualities of responsible *scientific* thought, why ought we not to suspect that *further* revisions may be in order to take adequate account of the actualities of good *theological* thought? "Very good," smiles the satyr face of Socrates, "muse on!"

This is an important exchange, it seems to me. One of the most significant kinds of aid that analytical philosophy can give to Christian thinking is precisely this sort of challenging encouragement to independent analyses that will do justice both to good logic and to the Christian form of life.

Such analyses, when developed, will of course insist that there are important logical differences as well as parallels between theories about the "spin of electrons" and theories about the "love of God." Let me illustrate. Both are similar in being only indirectly related to the world of ordinary experience; but it is possible to show,

108

I believe, that the nature of the indirection is different in kind. Both are similar in having a kind of factual significance that is to be carefully distinguished from the sort of factuality involved in talk about the "spin of the football" or the "love of Mr. Brown"; but there is certainly no rule requiring that two things distinguishable from a third thing are indistinguishable from one another. Both are similar in that they gain concreteness of interpretation for their nonempirical theoretical terms from associated imagery which functions as a theoretical "model"; but the logical status of the "model" relative to the "theory" is actually reversed in the two cases, since well-confirmed theories in science must take priority over even the best of scientific models, while in theology theories (despite their importance) come and go more readily than the basic value-focusing model imagery that defines the faith itself.

These are only a few hints, I acknowledge, about the sorts of things I believe will emerge once the Socratic challenge is accepted. I hope you are tantalized.[4] If I am to be cast in the role of analytic philosopher, I may as well attempt to don the mask of lure and stimulant that I am attempting to portray. If you have begun to hear the flutes for yourselves, my work thus far is a success.

[4] For the development of these ideas, see my *Basic Modern Philosophy of Religion* (New York: Scribner's, 1967), chaps. 12, 13, and 14.

Enough, then, for theological discourse. I suggest that it may well repay Christian thinkers to consider it under the aspect of a distinctive form of theoretical speech—one that is given concrete and vivid empirical interpretation by highly valued organizing images drawn from the scriptural tradition preserved and interpreted by the church. But what of this imagery itself? For Christians, access to an adequate picture of God is only through the Christ: "He who has seen me has seen the Father." "No one comes to the Father, but by me." And at this point we are inevitably thrown back on the need for an analysis of christological language. Where does the Socratic flute lead here?

We have already seen that a naïve equation of the "Christ of faith" with the critically confirmable "Jesus of history" rests on a logical confusion. But to what extent does it *matter* that our few historically reliable statements about Jesus, one of the many crucified by Pontius Pilate, do not lend themselves to religious commitment or to a particularly inspiring representation of the nature of God? Van A. Harvey wrestles with this question, too, in the final chapter of the book I mentioned earlier. His answer is to discriminate the various meanings of "Jesus of Nazareth" and to distinguish between (1) Jesus as he "really was," (2) Jesus as critical history can responsibly speak about him via warranted inferences from present data, (3) Jesus as "perspectival image," i.e., a paradigm figure through whom a glimpse of the meaning of human life may be gained, and (4) Jesus as interpreted theologically by the early church, the "Christ of faith," or (since this is what is portrayed) the biblical Christ. Of those four, Harvey finds the crucial and too often overlooked Jesus to be the illuminating perspectival image. There is no need to rule out the possibility of links, of course, between the biblical constructions and memory images of Jesus "as he really was." But hypotheses about these links, and associated speculations over the degree to which the Christian picture of Jesus is authentic to the man as he really was, are not the main issue. The primary question, christologically, is, as Harvey says, "whether the witness is a true one, that is, whether the last power with which men have to do can be trusted." [5]

The suggestion, then, is that the truth of faith—the justification of the central organizing images that constitute the Christian model—is not necessarily dependent on the truth of history. Harvey goes on:

Indeed, if we understand properly what is meant by faith, then this faith has no clear relation to any particular set of historical beliefs at all. Faith has to do with one's confidence in God, which is to say, with one's surrender of his attempts to establish his own righteousness and his acceptance of his life and creation as a gift and a responsibility. It is trust and commitment. This awareness, to be

[5] *The Historian and the Believer*, pp. 272-73.

sure, may be linked in the minds of some people with certain historical beliefs, but it is by no means clear that it must necessarily be so linked. Indeed, it could be argued that the history of the Christian church—not to mention the histories of those outside of the church—indicates that countless members of that body of belief have perceived this truth in and through stories that are, judged by modern criteria, mythological, which is to say, factually untrue.[6]

The language of the determinative Christian model, that is, is not to be justified by the kind of data and warrants appropriate to critical history, though the vividness of key Christian imagery is dependent on its being the sort of subject matter that might have been observed in history.

How, then, is this kind of language to be assessed? Harvey distinguishes between two logically different sort of subject matter that might have been observed in the perspectival image pictures him, and the belief that the perspectival image does illumine our experience and our relationship to that upon which we are absolutely dependent." [7] The vital consideration, in other words, is the power of the christocentric model to "illumine," or, as Harvey himself puts it, it has to do with "the adequacy of an image for interpreting the structure and

[6] *Ibid.*, p. 280.
[7] *Ibid.*, p. 282.

character of reality itself." [8] In the concreteness and particularity of specific images, so the gospel proclaims, something universally adequate for concrete and particular human lives is mediated.

Harvey's proposal is, I think, an excellent example of the stimulus provided by analytical philosophy, wearing Socrates' second face, when it joins in the christological dialogue. Not all problems are solved, of course. First, I fear that Harvey fails to take with sufficient seriousness the tenuousness of the warrants and the elusiveness of the data that might give support to claims, on behalf of various images, that they are more or less "adequate" for "interpreting the structure and character of reality itself." Moreover, models cannot perform this function alone with any significant degree of adequacy; it is only when models are given articulation by some theoretical structure that critical thinking can even begin the vital job (as Harvey puts it),

of attempting to demonstrate that a given perspective has a viability, intelligibility, and comprehensiveness that the alternative perspectives do not, that it is less eccentric, better able to account for those experiences and structures to which the alternatives attach special weight, as well as for those elements the alternatives seem to ignore or take no notice of.[9]

[8] *Ibid.*
[9] *Ibid.*, p. 285.

113

Even the implicit assumption that decision procedures are available by which these judgments can critically be made is not at all obvious, though I happen to believe that criteria can be dimly discerned if one looks with great care and applies them with great caution. Still, this must be argued with more care. And, finally, even if christological model and theological theory are appraised by the best means available and found "weakly" adequate (it would, I presume, require a considerable number of significant reforms in Christian orthodoxy for this to be possible), there still remains the problem of the comparable alternatives. They, too, may be capable of reform and of providing high and healthful meaning for human lives seeking perspective. Our theoretical decision procedures, supposing we find some, may not be able to discriminate one *and only one* "best" ultimate perspective. How shall we tip the balance? Given theoretical ambiguity, how shall we guide our lives?

Has language analysis anything positive to offer in this situation? Has language analysis, indeed, anything of a positive position to offer at all to inform Christian thinking, or are both faces of Socrates finally empty and mocking? I shall end my lecture with a serious consideration of this question, because it seems to me that the very notion of philosophy as "resource" for Christian thought is an ambiguous and potentially misleading one.

114

III

There is widespread—and ancient—supposition that the "constructive" or "positive" value of philosophy is to be measured solely by its provision of what I have here called theories and models for the representation of the "structure and character of reality itself." Certainly this is the possibility that is most exciting for Christians about "process" metaphysics and "existentialist" visions of man in the universe. But language analysis, so runs the common complaint, has no comparable vision of its own to offer. It only criticizes what others create—and, at best, acts as a goad and lure to constantly better creativity within the fields it criticizes. What kind of "resource" is this? Has analytical philosophy no wisdom of its own to offer?

Again I am struck with the extent to which language analysis stands, today, squarely in the Socratic tradition of philosophy. Since Socrates heard this criticism many times, it is instructive to note how he met it: by claiming only the role of midwife for assisting in bringing to healthy life the conceptions of others. As he is depicted as expressing it in Plato's *Theaetetus*:

I am so far like the midwife, that I cannot myself give birth to wisdom; and the common reproach is true, that, though I question others, I can myself bring nothing to light because there is no wisdom in me. The reason is this:

115

heaven constrains me to serve as a midwife, but has debarred me from giving birth. So of myself I have no sort of wisdom, nor has any discovery ever been born to me as the child of my soul.

But this acknowledged—this heaven-sent—barrenness is not mere negativity. Far from it!

Those who frequent my company at first appear, some of them, quite unintelligent; but, as we go further with our discussion, all who are favored by heaven make progress at a rate that seems surprising to others as well as to themselves, although it is clear that they have never learnt anything from us; the many admirable truths they bring to birth have been discovered by themselves from within. But the delivery is heaven's work and mine.

But this work, though modest, is not to be despised.

The proof of this is that many who have not been conscious of my assistance but have made light of me, thinking it was all their own doing, have left me sooner than they should . . . and thence forward suffered miscarriage of their thoughts through falling into bad company.

It does have its perils, however, as Socrates warns Theaetetus in advance:

Perhaps when I examine your statements I may judge one or another of them to be an unreal phantom. If I then take the abortion from you and cast it away, do not be savage with me like a woman robbed of her first child. People have often felt like that towards me and been positively ready to bite me for taking away some foolish notion they have conceived. They do not see that I am doing them a kindness. They have not learnt that no divinity is ever ill-disposed towards man, nor is such action on my part due to unkindness; it is only that I am not permitted to acquiesce in falsehood and suppress the truth.

To have such a midwife available, then, is a considerable resource. But for it to be a help does presuppose, at a minimum, that one's soul not be virginal. The unfruitful soul has no need for the midwife's art, and so should go get pregnant somewhere else. With this in mind Socrates adds to his list of the midwife's functions the untraditional skill of matchmaking. It is evident, as Socrates says, that

there are some, Theaetetus, whose minds, as I judge, have never conceived at all. I see that they have no need of me and with all goodwill I seek a match for them. . . . I have arranged many of these matches with Prodicus, and with other men of inspired sagacity.

I hope that the possible irony in Socrates' mention of Prodicus, one of the more prominent of the self-styled "wise men" or Sophists, will not rub off on my present

117

remarks. Those who offer us wisdom today are not Sophists in any pejorative sense.

Still, it is important to note the long persistence of two quite different sorts of resource for human thinking: there is the resource of the wise man, the seer, the provider of answers and comprehensive theories; and there is the resource of the lover (not to be confused with the confident possessor) of wisdom, the midwife, the nurse of truth.

Both are needed. The midwife has no role to play when mental wombs are empty. The seer without the midwife, however, may suppose himself great with child when he is only puffed up. I have no patience, therefore, for those who claim to see no positive use for language analysis simply because this deeply Socratic philosophic tradition does not itself give birth to metaphysical models and theories. Nor do I have more patience for analytical philosophers who fail to show the proper Socratic good will for those of "inspired sagacity" and who omit the matchmaking function from the definition of midwife. *"Both* seers and satyrs," is my motto.

Very well, but the question may be raised: Which is the more important sort of role for philosophy to play in any given historical situation? Which is for the sake of which? And, similarly, which face of Socrates is the more important one? My answer to the latter question, first, can by now be brief: both faces of Socrates—the numbing torpedo fish and the evocative satyr—are really his, but the first is always for the sake of the second. And likewise, language analysis, if it is playing its full philosophic role, will always put its criticisms (which it dare not neglect) into the context of continual calls for better and better independent thinking on the part of those who bear the brunt of destructive analysis. Similarly, like Socrates, language analysts should be alert to offer suggestions, possibilities, analogies, and hypotheses for consideration and assistance in this dialectical process.

Yes, but what of our other, more basic question of the priorities, at this present moment in history, between the Socratic and the seer traditions of philosophy? The simple—and some think the final—answer is that each one does philosophy as it is given to him to do, "as heaven constrains" him. Perhaps, they say, there is no getting behind our historical fatedness in order to argue with the gods who have decreed that some shall bear and that some shall assist in the bearing.

But there is, I believe, another word that can be added, and a word that is worth adding if men can to some degree transcend their histories. It is simply this: We, like Socrates, are living in a time of transition, when the old order is crumbling but the yearning for an heir to the new has yet to be met. At such a time many will appear with visions and images, but woe to us if we succumb too soon to our longing for closure.

We are living in a time for the disciplining of ourselves to sympathetic tentativeness when faced with comprehensive theories and ultimate images.

Most Christians are not used to this sensation of suspension, of irony, of living within acknowledged ambiguities—although much of the best in Christian tradition is fully compatible with such a stance—and therefore it is especially vital, I think, that Christian thought right now be increasingly intimate in dialogue with the heirs of Socrates. If Christians, therefore, are to heed that section of the Lord's Prayer asking not to be "led into temptation," they will—so far as they can transcend their own histories—lean toward the pole of Socratic irony. The other pole of philosophical resource is too easy, too natural, too comfortably in keeping with premature closure before the full newness of the present age has a chance to penetrate the intuitions, to inform the very bones of modern Christians. It is too easy for minds that have grown content with familiar organizing images and fairly adequate metaphysical theories to grow careless or even hostile toward new data or aspects of experience that do not quite fit cherished schemes. My plea is that current thought remain open, as far as possible, to the pole of adequacy: that is, to human experience in its present richness and variety as well as in its full historical depth. Since this openness to adequacy goes contrary to much human inclination toward the comforts of closure, the Socratic gadfly is, I believe, more than ever our painful friend.

But, finally, how does one live—can one live—suspended, without metaphysical or theological closure? Does the Socratic tradition not realize that men inevitably lean on organizing images for their values, whether they profess them or not? Have you not overlooked the need, I may be asked, for fruitful life in "the time being"?

I reply: Have you not seen? Have you not heard? Throughout the lecture I have been consciously displaying and commending an organizing image I believe to be both adequate for life and a persistent warning against the dangers of uncriticized closure.

It is, of course, the image of Socrates himself. In him I find a man who lived reverently, accepting his life as a divine gift and responsibility; in him I find a man who lived socially, accepting the sanctity of law while pursuing his obligation to question the specific legislative acts of men and to live, or die, by the primal law of his integrity before the best truth available. But in the image of Socrates I find not so much a cosmic metaphor as a possible paradigm—historical or not, it makes little difference—for a life to be lived with seriousness, zest, and responsible richness in an era properly suspicious of metaphysical models.

Language analysis and Christian thought? In the

end it comes back to the archetypical figures of Socrates and Jesus. Could the ironic old satyr and the passionate young seer have understood—and loved—each other? I suspect so, though their disciples in Athens and Jerusalem seem, alas, to have a much harder time of it.

5 | John Macquarrie   Existentialism and Christian Thought

Because theology is an attempt to bring to expression the content of faith, and because faith, in turn, is awakened by experiences of grace and revelation, it would seem that theology must always have peculiarities that separate it from what are called the "secular" disciplines. And yet, insofar as theology claims to be in some sense a science, an ordered intellectual investigation, it claims some kinship with the whole range of inquiries that make up the intellectual enterprise of mankind. Though the theologian bases himself on faith and revelation, as he has learned these in a community of faith, he must talk about language, history, man, and many other topics that are treated by other investigators besides himself, and if he is not to talk in a vacuum, as it were, but is to let his own insights contribute to the total human understanding and, where need be, to challenge some elements in it, then he has got to pay attention to what people in other disciplines are saying and try to relate his findings to theirs. The modern theologian has to try to relate himself to a very wide range of other scholars indeed—historians, sociologists, psychologists, natural scientists, and many others; yet perhaps the most important dialogical partner is still the one who has stood near at hand from the very beginnings of Christian theology —the philosopher. Sometimes we do come across theologians who, in reaction against some distortion of the relation between philosophy and theology, impatiently declare that they are through with the philosopher. Yet they soon drift back, or the next generation drifts back, or perhaps the truth is that they never really got away from some entanglement with the philosopher.

What does the theologian expect from the philosopher? Certainly, he should not expect the philosopher to do his work for him. Only if we do not believe that there is a genuine theological discipline anymore, that is to say, if we have given up faith and ceased to believe that there is any revelation, do we attempt to put a philosophy in the place of theology. In former times, it was often a metaphysical system that got substituted for theology, though the traditional Christian language might still be used to cast some kind of sanctity over the metaphysics. Nowadays, it is more likely to be a social ethic that will be substituted for theology, though it will retain the Christian moral ideal and its concrete exemplification in Jesus Christ. When the true task of theology is forgotten and gets swallowed up in metaphysics and ethics, then the relation of theology to philosophy has become perverted, and theologians have to assert anew the autonomy of their subject. Equally, of course, the philosopher has to ensure that his discipline is not turned into the handmaid of theology, and the memory of how this has indeed occurred at times in the past may partly account for the strongly lay and even anticlerical attitudes to be found in many philosophical schools today.

A true relation between philosophy and theology would respect the autonomy of each discipline. This means that the relation between them could not be a onesided one. In a dialogue with the philosopher in which both partners' integrity is preserved, the theologian must expect criticism as well as support. If he hopes that philosophy will allow him to clarify some areas of his own thinking and to strengthen some links in his own argument, he must also expect that philosophy will bring to his notice problems that he had overlooked and will show up weakness in his thinking of which he had been unaware. A fruitful relation between the theologian and the philosopher will include tensions as well as alliances, and perhaps it is in the give and take of this kind of dialogue that creative theologizing will take place.

But where in the philosophical world of our time is the theologian to find this dialogical partner? Many philosophers today seem to be talking about matters that, on the surface at least, seem very far from the interests of the theologian. Even at the beginning of the century, philosophers usually got around in their books to saying something about the ultimate nature of things, the existence of God, the final destiny of the human person, and such like. *Appearance and Reality, The Value and Destiny of the Individual, A Faith That Enquires, The World and the Individual*—these are typical titles of the important philosophical books being written fifty or sixty years ago, and even their titles would seem to indicate a relevance to theology. But if we pick up the volume *Philosophy in America*[1] published in 1965 and purporting to give a representative impression of the work of younger American philosophers at the present time, the titles that we meet are "Expressing," "On the Complexity of Avowals," "Must Every Inference Be Either Inductive or Deductive?" "Aesthetic Problems of Modern Philosophy," "Seeing Surfaces and Physical Objects," and so on. It so happens that I was asked to review this volume for a theological journal, and was really quite hard pressed to find in it something that I thought might be of interest to the average reader of theological journals! Certainly it is quite possible to be a very good philosopher nowadays without ever dealing with what used to be called "the great problems." So when today's theologian seeks to engage the philosopher in dialogue, it is quite likely that he will find that the philosopher just is not there. The philosopher has found new interests and new problems that have no obvious

[1] Essays, ed. by Max Black. Muirhead Library of Philosophy (Ithaca, New York: Cornell University Press, 1965).

connection with what the theologian is talking about. Theologians of the past have talked with friendly philosophers and unfriendly philosophers, but perhaps the unkindest cut of all is left for the present-day theologian who finds that many philosophers are just not interested in talking with him at all.

Well, is the theologian just to admit the complete irrelevance of his discipline, so that he decides either to pursue it in isolation (and thereby become still more irrelevant) or else to abandon it and join the philosopher in talking about things that are nowadays held to be more interesting? Neither of these courses is possible, if we are staying with our assumption that there is a true and great task for theology, a task that roots it in faith on the one hand and joins it to the whole human intellectual enterprise on the other. So it seems to me that the theologian must look again at the prevailing situation in philosophy and see if there is any point at which a dialogue might begin.

One thing we do notice about the philosophical world of today is its fragmentation. There are many different schools with very different ideas of what philosophy is all about and how it should be done. Do we find somewhere a place for a creative exchange between theology and philosophy? I believe myself that there are several such places. Some theologians have looked to the small group of philosophers who still interest themselves in metaphysics, in the tradition of the process philosophy of Whitehead and Hartshorne; others are having exchanges with those analytic philosophers who have shown an interest in the problems of religious language; others are appropriating the techniques of phenomenology for the theological problematic. In this lecture we shall be concerned with the dialogue between theology and existentialism. I do not think that any one of these approaches can make an exclusive claim. In our pluralistic culture, there are probably several valid ways of doing both philosophy and theology. I do not think either that a mixing of styles, an eclecticism, is very helpful to the theologian. He has to look for the kind of dialogue that will be, in his opinion, most fruitful and will reach the largest number of people, and then develop the possibilities of this dialogue as far as he can. So we select existentialism as the kind of philosophy that will make it possible for an interdisciplinary dialogue to get off the ground, as it were, and then we shall see how far it can reach.

Perhaps as a matter of fact existentialism is the type of philosophy that is most influential with theologians today. The early Barth, Bultmann, Tillich, and many other outstanding theologians of the last generation were deeply affected by it, and it continues to work strongly among contemporary theologians, both Catholic and Protestant, such as Rahner, Ott, Buri, and Ebeling, to name only a few of the better known.

It is not easy to characterize existentialism briefly, for it is not a body of doctrine but a way of doing philosophy. It is the way of philosophizing that begins from man himself, in his concrete existing as a being-in-the-world. The existentialist does not look to nature for the key to an understanding of the world, for man can be only a spectator over against nature and see its phenomena from the outside. His own existence, on the other hand, is something in which he participates at first hand and so something that he can know in a more direct and intimate way than the world of natural phenomena. But we should notice that this human existent is not conceived by the existentialists as primarily a thinking subject, so that it would be wrong to characterize existentialism as a form of subjectivism. The existent is, as we have already said, a being-in-the-world, and he only exists in his encounter with that which is other than himself. Furthermore, when man turns from the contemplation of the nature that lies outside him to analyze his own existing, it is not another "nature" that confronts him, so that he could list its properties, but the elusive, dynamic experience of an agent that is characterized by freedom, incompleteness, and risk.

I suppose that existentialism could be called a "secular" philosophy, at least in a fairly basic sense of that very imprecise word. If the secular is that which belongs in time and history, then existentialism is par excellence the philosophy of the secular, for the existence of which it speaks has a radically temporal and historical character. Yet existentialism is by no means a positivism. Because it begins from direct participation in the freedom and creativity of existence, it cuts behind the impasse into which the positivist falls.

Perhaps the first obvious point of contact between existentialism and Christian theology is that both offer a doctrine of man. If contemporary philosophy has turned away from speculative problems, such as the existence of God, so that it seems less ready to provide a dialogue with theology, this fact may be a useful reminder to the theologian that Christian theology is also anthropology, or that perhaps we should even speak of "theanthropology." Christian theology does not talk of God in himself, but of God in his relation to man, and the Christian faith is as much an understanding of man as it is of God. So perhaps a contemporary theology, so far as it adopts an apologetic style, should begin with the doctrine of man rather than with the more conventional starting point of the doctrine of God. The Christian existentialist does in fact follow this procedure and tries to unfold the meaning of Christian faith in terms of a description of a Christian existence. Obviously this does help to get Christian theology off the ground in a secular age. The question "Who is man?" is still asked when the question about God seems to have faded into the background. It may be the case, of course, that these two questions are so closely intertwined that one implies the other. Nevertheless, there are many conflicting answers to the question about man today, ranging from the plain unthinking hedonism that gets simply assumed to the highly subtle theories of Marxism and Freudianism. Christianity, interpreted as an understanding of man's existence in the world, can gain a certain relevance and can demand to be considered alongside other ways of understanding man, so that it may be judged, appreciated, accepted, or rejected in comparison with them.

Furthermore, existentialism offers to the theologian the resource of a language in which the structure of a Christian existence can be described. Whatever else one may say about the existentialists, it must surely be acknowledged that they have developed through their analyses a terminology that describes the basic characteristics of human existence in a remarkably full and precise manner. For this reason their work has proved just as helpful to psychoanalysts as to theologians. In the Bible and in traditional Christian theology, the doctrine of man is obscured by an antiquated and quasi-mythological terminology. In the Old Testament we hear of man's being compounded of the dust of the ground and the breath of life; while the apostle Paul, in spite of his penetrating insights into the meaning of Christian existence, has to express himself with such imprecise and antiquated terms as "flesh," "spirit," "heart," and the like.[2] Existentialism offers an accurate and up-to-date vocabulary in which to express this biblical understanding of man.

But existentialism provides much more than a vocabulary. Language needs syntax as well as vocabulary, for individual words are fully meaningful only as parts of larger wholes. Existentialism not only provides terms, but also wider principles of interpretation and articulation. The biblical terms themselves have their home, so to speak, in wider contexts of myth, of history, of cultic and legal institutions, or whatever it may be. Bultmann's demythologizing is the best known example of the application of existential interpretation to wider areas of the biblical material, but this is only part of the problem of interpretation. The so-called "new hermeneutic" has sought to probe further into the problems of interpretation, and existential philosophy continues to play an important role in its procedures.

But is an existential interpretation of the biblical material valid? Some people would say that what is happening is that a modern philosophy is being imposed upon the traditional Christian material and that its substance is quietly got rid of. I do believe that this style of interpretation and of theologizing can, like any other, become one-sided and so distorting. Perhaps the risk of

[2] See "Existentialism and the Christian Vocabulary" in my *Studies in Christian Existentialism, Lectures and Essays* (Philadelphia: The Westminster Press, 1966).

132

such distortion has to be taken in every reinterpretation of Christian truth, yet if there is no reinterpretation, that truth becomes inaccessible to us. Perhaps too there is a legitimate place for violence in interpretation, for the person originally using the words was probably not himself aware of all the implications contained in them, and it is the business of the interpreter to bring out these hidden implications, though they may sometimes be startling.

Yet I would claim that the interpretation of the biblical material in terms of contemporary existentialist philosophy is, within limits, justifiable. For this philosophy does seem to have sufficient affinity with the biblical outlook to ensure that it does not force the biblical teaching into an alien mold. Just as the Bible view of creation sees man occupying a distinctive place in it, so the existentialist views him as standing out from the inanimate world and from the animal world; just as the Bible sees polarities in man, symbolized by the dust of the ground and the breath of life, or by flesh and spirit, so the existentialist is aware of the tension between man's freedom and his finitude, his responsibility and his guilt, and so on; and again, just as the Bible speaks of faith, so the existentialist sees the need for man to take up attitudes in the world without the possibility of verifying them in advance. Perhaps above all, existentialism agrees with the Bible in stressing the priority and distinctiveness of the personal.

But what about God in all this? Is existentialism simply a humanism, as Sartre claims? Does the existential interpretation of Christianity finally fall into the category of an immanentist ethical interpretation, which we have already acknowledged to be not really an interpretation but a substitute for the Christian faith? [3]

It is clear that Bultmann did not think of himself as replacing traditional Christian faith by a philosophy of existence, and he explicitly says so himself.[4] On the other hand, existentialism by its very nature does not offer any proof of God's existence and does not develop any metaphysic that would try to show the relations of God, man, and the world within an all-embracing whole. What Christian existentialism does is to draw attention to those features of existence at which men begin to talk of God. In other words, if existentialism does not offer any proof of God's existence, at least it shows us the kind of experiences that give rise to God-talk. It is at this point perhaps that one can see the convergence between existentialism and logical analysis, as far as their bearing upon religion and theology is concerned.[5] Just as Wittgenstein insisted that language must be studied in

[3] See above, p. 124.
[4] Cf. *Kerygma and Myth,* ed. by H. W. Bartsch, trans. by R. H. Fuller (London: S.P.C.K., 1953), pp. 23 ff.
[5] Cf. J. A. Martin, Jr., *The New Dialogue Between Philosophy and Theology* (New York: The Seabury Press, 1966), p. 203.

its context of use, so the existentialist relates language to the human situations to which it gives expression. For this reason we mentioned earlier that, in an existential analysis, talk of God is always at the same time talk about ourselves. We talk of God only insofar as we experience his acting upon us. This does not mean that God has been subjectivized or reduced to a factor in human existence. In experiences both of grace and judgment, the Christian existentialist believes himself to be confronted and affected by a reality that transcends his own —and I think this would hold even for Herbert Braun, who is probably the most seemingly subjectivist of existential theologians, and who has been held to come close to an atheistic position. Of course all existential theologians would acknowledge the risk of faith. We see things only from the side of human existence. We cannot *prove* that what we call "God" is indeed a reality that transcends us. We have faith that this is indeed the case, for we believe that we experience the priority of God in his grace and revelation, but in the long run this might be an illusion.

However, I think some existentialists would go further and claim that their faith is a reasonable faith. Existentialism need not be merely quixotic, and faith, though it cannot be knowledge, need not remain a leap in the dark. Some existentialists are prepared to go on to sketch out an ontology. Berdyaev claimed that, while

Kant and modern philosophy may have discredited the
metaphysics of the object, they have not discredited
what he calls the "metaphysics of the subject." This last
expression is a rather unfortunate one, but it is clarified
when Berdyaev tells us that in his view metaphysics
must be constructed by the whole man.[6] I would prefer
myself to talk of "existential ontology," that is to say, an
understanding of being that is developed on the basis
of the existential understanding of one's own being-in-
the-world, rather than a rational speculative metaphysic
in the old style. The precedent for this advance from a
pure existentialism to an existential ontology is, of course,
set by Martin Heidegger. His early work was devoted
to the existential analysis of the human *Dasein*; but
already his sights were trained on Being in the widest
sense, and it is to the investigation of the question of
Being that his later work has been directly and explicitly
addressed.

Some existential theologians hesitate to move in
the direction of an ontology. Bultmann himself makes
use of the early work of Heidegger but shows little interest in the latter's ontological investigations. Yet it seems
to me that theology cannot dispense with an ontology.
Perhaps the suspicion that this word arouses in the
minds of some theologians is due to the fact that they

[6] *The Beginning and the End* (New York: Harper, 1957),
pp. 9, 37.

still understand the word in its traditional sense and see in the development of an ontology a retreat from the dynamic, historical concepts of existentialism back to a static notion of Being. But this would be to misunderstand the kind of ontology that Heidegger tries to develop. Being, as he conceives it, is not static. It is rather to be understood in terms analogous to the understanding of human existence itself, which was taken as the clue to the meaning of Being. Heidegger's notion of Being, like his notion of the self, leaves behind the categories of substantiality, derived from thinghood, and seeks new categories that will be derived from personal existence.

I have tried elsewhere[7] to show the bearing of Heidegger's later philosophy on Christian theology, and how in particular it supplies something like a modern counterpart to the old-fashioned and nowadays largely discredited natural theology. As has already been said, existentialism does not offer proofs, and so it does not claim to fulfill the role of a natural theology in that regard. But it does describe in its analyses the kinds of experience out of which faith in God arises, and insofar as it does this, it links God-talk with ordinary everyday talk and permits us to judge how legitimate or illegitimate such God-talk is.

[7] In my *Principles of Christian Theology* (New York: Scribner's, 1966), chaps. IV and V.

It seems to me that, beyond his analysis of human existence itself, there are at least two items in Heidegger's philosophy that can be very helpful to the theologian in setting up a conceptual structure in terms of which the foundations of religious faith can be explicated. The first of these Heideggerian doctrines is his account of primordial thinking—a kind of thinking that he opposes to calculative thinking and that is described as passive, meditative, open to Being. It is clear that such thinking affords a secular parallel to what the theologian calls "revelation." Heinrich Ott has also sought to draw out the similarities between Heidegger's view of thinking and this fundamental theological idea of revelation. The other point in Heidegger is his concept of Being. As he understands it, Being is not another being, but the condition that comes before every particular being. In a period when we must seek reformulations of theism, it seems to me that the Heideggerian concept of Being offers the possibility of a model for thinking of God. Actually, Tillich's way of talking about God lies very close to Heidegger's concept of Being. Such an idea of God not only escapes some of the objections that were so troublesome for the traditional notion of a substantial God beyond the beings, but also combines in a remarkable way the notions of transcendence and immanence, both of which are essential to any thought of God that is consonant with the Christian revelation. Actually, since this style of ontology is developed from the understand-

138

ing of being that is given in our own existence as personal beings, the God or divine Being whom it conceptualizes is, like the God of the Bible, very much a living God, to be conceived in dynamic, temporal terms analogous to those in which we conceive selfhood.

A contemporary apologetic consists as much as anything simply in the clarification of Christian faith. It is more concerned with interpreting meanings than with establishing proofs. It seems to me that existentialism and existential ontology succeed in doing this remarkably well.

When we turn away from the apologetic task and from the more theoretical type of theologizing to the service of theology within the church, I think it may be claimed once more that existentialism provides a very rich resource. It helps to link theology with proclamation and to show the relevance of Christian doctrine to the work of the preacher, as he seeks to conform the life of the church to the demands of the gospel. For a philosophy that arises out of the concrete experience of existing in the world comes back to this existence with a renewed and deeper understanding. In insisting that dogmas have to do with man and his life as well as with God, the existential approach prevents theology from straying into an abstract scholasticism and keeps it near to the life problems of the church.

Of course like every other theological method, this one has its difficulties. I can only mention some of these.

139

Does the existential-ontological approach lead into a kind of Gnosticism in which the concrete historical basis of the Christian faith is volatilized? Again, can a way of theologizing that centers so emphatically on man yield a theology of nature or an adequate doctrine of creation? Still more radically, is the analysis of man that emerges in existentialism one with universal validity, or does it not perhaps miss the mark when we consider the technological man of today? These are serious questions, but I believe that the existential theologian can answer them, and that his approach is sufficiently flexible to adapt itself to whatever valid criticisms might underlie these questions.

Let me again say that the existential theologian, if he is wise, does not claim a monopoly in the field of theology and does not fall into the error, so lamentably common, of saying "This is the only way." In our fragmented culture, there is no single valid way of doing either theology or philosophy. The most that a wise practitioner will claim is that his particular approach solves some problems and gains some insights in this time of change and confusion.

| Contributors

Frederick Ferré, Chairman, Department of Philosophy,
Dickinson College. Author of *Language,
Logic, and God,* and *Basic Modern Phi-
losophy of Religion.*

Charles Hartshorne, Ashbel Smith Professor of Philosophy, University of Texas. Author of
many books, among them: *Man's Vision
of God, The Divine Relativity, Reality as
Social Process, The Logic of Perfection,
Anselm's Discovery,* and *A Natural
Theology for Our Time.*

Quentin Lauer, S.J., Associate Professor of Philosophy,
Fordham University. Author of *Phénoménologie de Husserl: Essai sur la genèse de
l'intentionnalité;* and *The Triumph of
Subjectivity: An Introduction to Transcendental Phenomenology.* Translator of
Husserl's *Phenomenology and the Crisis
of Philosophy.*

141

Perry LeFevre, Academic Dean and Professor of Constructive Theology, Chicago Theological Seminary. Author of *The Prayers of Kierkegaard, The Christian Teacher, Understandings of Man.*

John Macquarrie, Professor of Systematic Theology, Union Theological Seminary. Author of *An Existentialist Theology, The Scope of Demythologization, Twentieth-Century Religious Thought, Principles of Christian Theology, Studies in Christian Existentialism, God-Talk.*